First World War
and Army of Occupation
War Diary
France, Belgium and Germany

41 DIVISION
124 Infantry Brigade
Royal Fusiliers (City of London Regiment)
32nd Battalion
1 May 1916 - 31 October 1917

WO95/2644/2

The Naval & Military Press Ltd
www.nmarchive.com
Published in association with The National Archives

Published by

The Naval & Military Press Ltd

Unit 10 Ridgewood Industrial Park,

Uckfield, East Sussex,

TN22 5QE England

Tel: +44 (0) 1825 749494

www.naval-military-press.com

www.nmarchive.com

This diary has been reprinted in facsimile from the original. Any imperfections are inevitably reproduced and the quality may fall short of modern type and cartographic standards.

© Crown Copyright
Images reproduced by permission of The National Archives, London, England, 2015.

Contents

Document type	Place/Title	Date From	Date To
Heading	WO95/2644/3		
Heading	41st Division 124th Infy Bde 32nd Bn Roy. Fus. May 1916 Oct 1917 To Italy 1917 Nov Disbanded March 1918.		
Heading	War Diary Of The 32nd Battalion Royal Fusiliers From 5th May 1916 To 31st May 1916. Volume 1.		
War Diary	Aldershot.	01/05/1916	04/05/1916
War Diary	Havre.	05/05/1916	06/05/1916
War Diary	Wallon Cappel.	07/05/1916	14/05/1916
War Diary	Meteren.	15/05/1916	30/05/1916
War Diary	Papot.	31/05/1916	31/05/1916
Heading	32nd (S) Bn The Royal Fusiliers War Diary June 1916. Vol. 2.		
War Diary	Papot.	01/06/1916	03/06/1916
War Diary	Ploegsteert	04/06/1916	11/06/1916
War Diary	Papot.	11/06/1916	16/06/1916
War Diary	Ploegsteert.	17/06/1916	23/06/1916
War Diary	Papot.	24/06/1916	30/06/1916
Heading	32nd (F) Bn The Royal Fusiliers War Diary July 1916. Vol. 3		
War Diary	Papot.	30/06/1916	30/06/1916
War Diary	Ploegsteert.	01/07/1916	10/07/1916
War Diary	Creslow.	11/07/1916	16/07/1916
War Diary	Ploegsteert.	17/07/1916	22/07/1916
War Diary	Papot.	23/07/1916	27/07/1916
War Diary	Ploegsteert.	28/07/1916	31/07/1916
Miscellaneous	Trench Raid.	09/07/1916	09/07/1916
War Diary	Ploegsteert.	01/08/1916	02/08/1916
War Diary	Greslow.	03/08/1916	08/08/1916
War Diary	Ploegsteert.	09/08/1916	16/08/1916
War Diary	Greslow.	17/08/1916	17/08/1916
War Diary	Lacreche.	18/08/1916	28/08/1916
War Diary	Bellancourt.	24/08/1916	01/09/1916
War Diary	In Billets.	01/09/1916	01/09/1916
War Diary	Camies E Of Abbevilles.	02/09/1916	07/09/1916
War Diary	Near Edge Hill Syn In Camp.	08/09/1916	08/09/1916
War Diary	(D.19.d. Mod Sheet 62.d).	09/09/1916	09/09/1916
War Diary	Near Fricourt (F.14.b. Map.)	10/09/1916	10/09/1916
War Diary	Sheet 62.d	11/09/1916	16/09/1916
War Diary	In Trenches	17/09/1916	17/09/1916
War Diary	Near Edge Hill Stn. Camp.	18/09/1916	18/09/1916
War Diary	(D.19.d. Map Sheet 62.D)	19/09/1916	24/09/1916
War Diary	Near Edge Hill Stn (Camp)	25/09/1916	30/09/1916
Miscellaneous	Operation Orders.	14/09/1916	14/09/1916
Miscellaneous			
Miscellaneous	Report On Operations On 15th, 16th & 17th September, 1916, Carried Out By 124th Infantry Brigade Near Flers.	20/09/1916	20/09/1916

Miscellaneous	The Following Points Were Brought To Notice During The Action' And Are Submitted As Suggested For the Consideration Of The G.O.C.		
War Diary	Near Edge Hill Stn Camp.	01/10/1916	02/10/1916
War Diary	Pomiers Redoubt.	03/10/1916	03/10/1916
War Diary	Support In Trenches	04/10/1916	05/10/1916
War Diary	Gird Support & Advanced Trenches.	06/10/1916	10/10/1916
War Diary	Mametz Wood Camp.	11/10/1916	11/10/1916
War Diary	Becordel Camp.	12/10/1916	13/10/1916
War Diary	Buire.	14/10/1916	16/10/1916
War Diary	Longpres	17/10/1916	19/10/1916
War Diary	Meteren Area.	20/10/1916	20/10/1916
War Diary	Patricia Camp.	21/10/1916	21/10/1916
War Diary	Ridgewood.	22/10/1916	26/10/1916
War Diary	Ridgewood Huts.	27/10/1916	27/10/1916
War Diary	Trenches.	28/10/1916	31/10/1916
War Diary	Vierstraat.	01/11/1916	03/11/1916
War Diary	La-Clytte.	04/11/1916	09/11/1916
War Diary	Vierstraat.	10/11/1916	15/11/1916
War Diary	Ridgewood.	16/11/1916	21/11/1916
War Diary	Vierstraat.	22/11/1916	27/11/1916
War Diary	La Clytte.	28/11/1916	30/11/1916
War Diary	Vierstraat.	01/12/1916	06/12/1916
War Diary	Ridgewood.	07/12/1916	12/12/1916
War Diary	Vierstraat.	13/12/1916	19/12/1916
War Diary	La Clytte.	20/12/1916	26/12/1916
War Diary	Vierstraat.	27/12/1916	31/12/1916
War Diary	Vierstraat.	01/12/1916	06/12/1916
War Diary	Ridgewood.	07/12/1916	12/12/1916
War Diary	Vierstraat.	13/12/1916	19/12/1916
War Diary	La Clytte.	20/12/1916	26/12/1916
War Diary	Vierstraat.	27/12/1916	31/12/1916
War Diary	Report Of Lt. Col. R.E. Key On The Raid Carried Out On Night 2/3rd December 1916.	03/12/1916	03/12/1916
Miscellaneous	Report On Raid 2/3rd Dec, 1916.		
Miscellaneous	Report On Raid 2/3rd December 1916.	03/12/1916	03/12/1916
Miscellaneous	Report On Nights Operations.	15/12/1916	15/12/1916
War Diary	Vierstraat.	01/01/1917	01/01/1917
War Diary	Ridge Wood.	02/01/1917	08/01/1917
War Diary	Vierstraat.	08/01/1917	14/01/1917
War Diary	La Clytte.	14/01/1917	20/01/1917
War Diary	Vierstraat.	20/01/1917	26/01/1917
War Diary	Ridge Wood.	26/01/1917	31/01/1917
War Diary	In The Line Vierstraat.	01/02/1917	04/02/1917
War Diary	La Clytte.	05/02/1917	09/02/1917
War Diary	Vierstraat.	10/02/1917	15/02/1917
War Diary	Ridgewood.	16/02/1917	21/02/1917
War Diary	Vierstraat.	22/02/1917	28/02/1917
War Diary	La Clytte.	28/02/1917	28/02/1917
Miscellaneous	Report Of Raid On Hollandscheschuur Salient By 10th Bn "Queens" R.W.S. 24th February, 1917.		
War Diary	La Clytte.	01/03/1917	05/03/1917
War Diary	Vierstraat In The Line.	06/03/1917	12/03/1917
War Diary	Ridge Wood.	13/03/1917	17/03/1917
War Diary	Ridgewood & Vierstraat.	18/03/1917	21/03/1917
War Diary	Steenvoorde.	22/03/1917	05/04/1917

Type	Location	From	To
War Diary	Reninghelst.	06/04/1917	07/04/1917
War Diary	Reninghelst (On Tario Camp).	08/04/1917	11/04/1917
War Diary	Reninghelst & Left Sector Of Steloi Sector.	12/04/1917	14/04/1917
War Diary	In The Line St Eloi Sector Left Sector.	15/04/1917	17/04/1917
War Diary	Reninghelst (Cihpiewa Camp).	18/04/1917	22/04/1917
War Diary	In The Line St Eloi Sector Left Sector.	23/04/1917	01/05/1917
War Diary	Chippewa "B" Reninghelst.	02/05/1917	03/05/1917
War Diary	Ontario & Micmac Camps.	04/05/1917	11/05/1917
War Diary	Chippewa "A".	12/05/1917	12/05/1917
War Diary	Chippewa "A" Camp.	13/05/1917	17/05/1917
War Diary	Abeele.	18/05/1917	18/05/1917
War Diary	Houlle.	19/05/1917	30/05/1917
War Diary	Middle Camp West.	31/05/1917	31/05/1917
Miscellaneous	A Form. Messages And Signals.		
War Diary	Middle Camp W.	01/06/1917	05/06/1917
War Diary	In The Line.	06/06/1917	07/06/1917
War Diary	Elzenwalle Camp.	08/06/1917	11/06/1917
War Diary	In Support To Right Bde Sector.	12/06/1917	15/06/1917
War Diary	Rt Sub Sector.	16/06/1917	22/06/1917
War Diary	In Support.	23/06/1917	26/06/1917
War Diary	Left Sub Sector.	27/06/1917	30/06/1917
Miscellaneous	Report On Operations. June 7th, 1917.	10/06/1917	10/06/1917
War Diary	Meteren.	01/07/1917	13/07/1917
War Diary	Ridgewood.	13/07/1917	13/07/1917
War Diary	Ridgewood.	14/07/1917	24/07/1917
War Diary	Ridgewood And De Zon Camp La Clytte.	25/07/1917	25/07/1917
War Diary	De Zon Camp La Clytte.	26/07/1917	29/07/1917
War Diary	De Zon Camp.	30/07/1917	30/07/1917
War Diary	Voormezeele.	30/07/1917	31/07/1917
Miscellaneous	32nd (S) Battn. The Royal Fusiliers.		
War Diary	G.H.Q. 2nd Line.	01/08/1917	03/08/1917
War Diary	Klein Zillebeke.	04/08/1917	09/08/1917
War Diary	Imperial Trench.	10/08/1917	14/08/1917
War Diary	Ridge Wood.	15/08/1917	15/08/1917
War Diary	Fletre.	15/08/1917	24/08/1917
War Diary	Staple.	25/08/1917	29/08/1917
War Diary	Tatinghem Area.	30/08/1917	13/09/1917
War Diary	Zuytpeene.	14/09/1917	14/09/1917
War Diary	Thieushouk.	15/09/1917	15/09/1917
War Diary	La Clytte.	16/09/1917	16/09/1917
War Diary	Ridge Wood.	17/09/1917	18/09/1917
War Diary	Canada Street Tunnels.	18/09/1917	22/09/1917
War Diary	Ridge Wood	23/09/1917	23/09/1917
War Diary	Castre Area.	23/09/1917	23/09/1917
War Diary	La Brearde.	24/09/1917	28/09/1917
War Diary	Ghyvelde.	29/09/1917	30/09/1917
Miscellaneous	Report On Operations 20th To 23rd September, 1917 32nd (S) Bn The Royal Fusiliers.	10/10/1917	10/10/1917
War Diary	Ghyvelde "B" Camp.	01/10/1917	05/10/1917
War Diary	Coxyde Bains.	06/10/1917	14/10/1917
War Diary	In The Line.	15/10/1917	23/10/1917
War Diary	Yorkshire Camp.	24/10/1917	27/10/1917
War Diary	Teteghem.	28/10/1917	31/10/1917

WO 95/26444/3

41ST DIVISION
124TH INFY BDE

32ND BN ROY. FUS.

MAY 1916 ~~MAR 1918~~ OCT 1917

TO ITALY 1917 NOV

DISBANDED MARCH 1918

CONFIDENTIAL
WAR DIARY
OF THE
32nd Battalion Royal Fusiliers
from 5th May 1916 TO 31st May 1916
VOLUME 1

Army Form C. 2118.

Sheet I
WAR DIARY
or
INTELLIGENCE SUMMARY
(Erase heading not required.)

32nd Royal Fusiliers

Instructions regarding War Diaries and Intelligence Summaries are contained in F. S. Regs., Part II and the Staff Manual respectively. Title Pages will be prepared in manuscript.

Place	Date	Hour	Summary of Events and Information	Remarks and references to Appendices
ALDERSHOT	1/5/16		Mobilisation	
"	2/5/16		do	
"	3/5/16		do	
"	4/5/16		Batt'n entrained in three trains at FARNBOROUGH for SOUTHAMPTON DOCKS. Arrived punctually & without any casualties. Strength 34 Officers 985 O.R. Bn. 10 men attached to 124th Inf Brigade's 41st Division. Sailed on S/S HELLEROPHON at 6.30 & S/S LYDIA at 6.30 & S/S MONAQUEEN at 7pm.	
HAVRE	5/5/16	1.30 a.m 7.30 a.m	Arrived at HAVRE. Voyage very quiet. Disembarked & marched to Rest Camp. N°2. Strength 34 Officers & 995 O.R.	
"	6/5/16	12.30 p.m 6.10 p.m	"D" Co entrained with 26th R. F. A.B.C. Cos at Pointe I HAVRE Station for HAZEBROUCK. Orderly Room Sergt N° 22292 Sergt CLARK reported to Base Commandant for duty with A.A.G. 3rd ECHELON Base. N° 22544 A.B&C Cos detrained at STEENBECQUE. Absentee L/Cpl Bruce (subsequently Court Rifles rejoined) "D" Co " " " " WALLON CAPPEL. C 85	
WALLON CAPPEL	7/5/16	3 pm	Marched about 3 miles to billets at WALLON CAPPEL.	

Army Form C. 2118.

Sheet II
WAR DIARY
or
INTELLIGENCE SUMMARY
(Erase heading not required.)

32nd Royal Fusiliers

Place	Date	Hour	Summary of Events and Information	Remarks and references to Appendices
HALLON CAPPEL	8/5/16		Batt's Route March. Circular route via SERCUS — about 7 miles. Continuous rain. No men fell out.	
	9/5/16	9 a.m.	2nd Lt SHAKESPEAR prepared list of billets showing numbers attached & handed to Major. Marched & new billets — in Brigade — between OUTTERSTEENE & METTEREN. Distance about 13 miles. Rain incessant. 2 Men fell out & reported again en route.	
	10/5/16		C.O. Organisation. C.O. Brief. Bayonet fighting &c under C.O. arrangements.	
	11/5/16	9.30 a.m.	All ranks received instruction in Gas Defence measures from Chemical Adviser 2nd Army at STRAZEEL.	
		2.30 p.m.	Bayonet fighting &c under C.O. arrangements.	
	12/5/16		Batt's Concentration March to FLETRE. Distance about 6 miles.	
			Interpreter M. J. TRIGHE reported for duty.	
	13/5/16	3.15 p.m.	C.O., 11 officers & 40 o.r. proceeded to 265 Inf. Brigade Reserve Billets, at for instruction in trench warfare with 10th A.& S. Highlanders.	
	14/5/16	8.30 a.m.	R.C. Church Parade at OUTTERSTEENE	
		11.0	C.ofE. Parade at T.S.H.Q.	
		10— 2 p.m.	Lectures on Lewis Gun to all ranks in C.O. area	

2449 Wt. W14957/M90 750,000 1/16 J.B.C. & A. Forms/C.2118/12.

… Army Form C. 2118.

SHEET 3.
WAR DIARY
INTELLIGENCE SUMMARY
(Erase heading not required.)

32nd ROYAL FUSILIERS

Place	Date	Hour	Summary of Events and Information	Remarks and references to Appendices
METEREN	1915 15	10.30 a.m.	7 Mile Concentration March.	
		10.30	Specialist Training	
		2 p.m.	Bayonet fighting under Co arrangements.	
— do —	16.5.16	9 a.m.	3rd Trench Party under Major C.P. Martin proceeded to PLOEGSTEERT trenches for instruction with 18th A & S. Highlanders.	
		9.15	Physical Drill	
		10.15	Company Drill	1st Trench Party returned. Casualties.
		11.15	Bayonet fighting under Co arrangements.	
		6 p.m.		
		8 p.m.	Night operations on BAILLEUL – STRAZEELE Rd.	2/Lt No 11743 Pte Kennedy accidentally wounded by a shot of C/Sgt Garner's Revolver.
— do —	17.5.16	6.30	Physical Drill	
		9 a.m.	C.O's Inspection. Lecture. Bayonet fighting. Bombing Practice.	
		9.15	Route March. STRAZEELE – MERRIS & return.	
		11–10	Emergency Mobilisation. (Practice). Ready to move off 12.15	
		9 p.m.	Bayonet fighting	
		10	Bombing	
— do —	18.5.16	12 noon	2nd Trench Party returned. Casualties Nil.	
		2 p.m.	Route March about 5 Miles	
— do —	19.5.16	9.15	Physical Drill	
		9.45	Bayonet fighting	
		11.30	Bombing	
		8 p.m.	Night March to FLETRE. Distance about 5 miles.	
— do —	20.5.16			

War Diary or Intelligence Summary

Army Form C. 2118.

SHEET 4.

Place	Date	Hour	Summary of Events and Information	Remarks and references to Appendices
METEREN	21/5/16	9 am 9.45 2.30 pm	Non-grant Church Parade C of E Batt'n Kit Inspection	Gazetting. Promotion to Lt of 2nd Lts PILGRIM. THORTBURN LAYER appeared in Lon: Gazette 10/5/16.
— do —	22/5/16	9.15 9.45 10.30 11.30 7.30	Physical Drill Bayonet Fighting Bomb'g & Squad Drill Bomb'g Drill Physical Drill	No. 22166 Sergt Penning proceeded to Army Warfare School on Sniping Junk.
— do —	23/5/16	9 10.30 12 7.30 pm 9 am	Bombing Musketry Lewis Gun Junks Route March C.O.'s Inspection. All Coys on Coy Parade Grounds.	C.O. Commanders Conference at B.H.Q. Coy Commanders Conference at B.H.Q.
— do —	24/5/16		Normal Training Programme.	
— do —	25/5/16	2.15 11.30	Normal Training Programme Brigade Signallers. Practice of Emergency Move. Practiced ready to move off at 1.30 a.m. incl. Transport.	Prizgiven. ME!
— do —		4.15	Athletic Sports. 26th R.F.	
— do —	26/5/16		Normal Training Programme Bath 2nd B.C. Coy at METEREN.	Major C.P. Hastings promoted to substantive rank of Lieut Col. Gazette. 20/5/16.

WAR DIARY / INTELLIGENCE SUMMARY

Army Form C. 2118.

(Erase heading not required.)

Place	Date	Hour	Summary of Events and Information	Remarks and references to Appendices
METEREN	27-5-16	6.30 a.m. 9.30 3 pm	Bayonet fighting Route March. Croaken Mont via OUTTERSTENE & BAILLEUL. Gen. held will meet CO. commandants	
	29-5-16	9.30 a.m.	Inspection by G.O.C. 12th Inf. Brigade. Very successful parade. Lecture on 1st Aid by M.O. Usual afternoon Training Programme.	2nd Lt. A. CLAPTON reported at 6.30 p.m. 2nd Lt. W. SHART (Brig. Res.)
	28-5-16	9.45 6 " 9.30	Church Parades. C.E. M.C. R.C.h.	
		2.15 6.15 8 P.O.	Usual Training Programme. Afternoon employed packing. Match: LE CRECHE Billets (Bn. m. matthew) vs Billets.	2nd Lt. W. SHART proceeded to ENGLAND. (2nd Army A/1913/43 9/27/5/16) Attached { } 30-6-16
	30-5-16			
PAPOT	31-5-16	3.15 am 8 "	Left LE CRECHE for PAPOT. Distance about 8 miles. Bn. arrived at shut camp at PAPOT. Delayed in rear & Bullet by Brigade. Remainder of day spent cleaning up etc. Took over Camp from 10th A.D.S. Highlanders.	
			Lt. G.W. BAGOT 2nd Lt. H.G. NOBLE 2nd Lt. E.V. CLARK } 19th R.F. reported for duty from Base at ETAPLES 2nd Lt. BARKER - 11th H.L.O. & _____	Strength O.R. 982 Officers 37

32nd (S) Bn The Royal Fusiliers

War Diary

June 1916

Army Form C. 2118.

WAR DIARY
or
INTELLIGENCE SUMMARY

(Erase heading not required.)

32nd Royal Fusiliers.

Place	Date	Hour	Summary of Events and Information	Remarks and references to Appendices
PAPOT	1/6/16	6.30 9.15 10.15 11.30	Physical Drill Bayonet Fighting Platoon & Squad Drill Bombing	
"	2/6/16		Usual Programme T. work.	
"	3/6/16		do	
PLOEGST	4/6/16	5 a.m.	Relieved 11th R.W. Kents in Plug St Trenches. T.121.122.123. Relief complete 7.30 a.m. On our left 26th T.T. On our right 21st K.R.R. Uneventful day & night.	
"	5/6/16		Everything normal. G.O.C 41st Division visited Battn H.Q.	
"	7/6/16		do	
"	8/6/16		Aerial & Artillery activity. Everything normal otherwise.	

Army Form C. 2118.

WAR DIARY
or
INTELLIGENCE SUMMARY

(Erase heading not required.)

Instructions regarding War Diaries and Intelligence Summaries are contained in F. S. Regs., Part II. and the Staff Manual respectively. Title Pages will be prepared in manuscript.

Place	Date	Hour	Summary of Events and Information	Remarks and references to Appendices
PLOEG-STEERT	9/6/16	3 p-	Artillery Bombardment in afternoon between BIRDCAGE being object. Results unsatisfactory. G.O.C. 124th Inf. Brigade arrived at B.H.Q.	
		8 p-		
	10/6/16	3 p - 5 p-	Arranged O. arrant for German retaliation with Whiz Bang &c. Preceding day Bombardment. Heavy Trench Mortars at BIRDCAGE at G.O.C. 144th Inf. Brigade obliged to cold whilst visiting trenches slightly.	
	11/6/16	5 a-	End of Jonathan covered around of Brigade in the absence.	
PAPOT			Relieved by 11th R.W.K. & returned to PAPOT. Casualties for week to Men wounded Duty 1 accidentally.	
	12/6/16		Usual Training Programme. "C" Coy Baths. No working parties.	
	13/6/16		do – usual working parties.	
	14/6/16		do –	

Army Form C. 2118.

WAR DIARY
or
INTELLIGENCE SUMMARY
(Erase heading not required.)

Instructions regarding War Diaries and Intelligence Summaries are contained in F. S. Regs., Part II. and the Staff Manual respectively. Title Pages will be prepared in manuscript.

Place	Date	Hour	Summary of Events and Information	Remarks and references to Appendices
PAPOT	15/6/16		Usual Training Programme interfered with by Working parties. G.O.C. (C in C) Fourter inspected bivouack. Application for trentin Defence scheme refused with order interfere with weekly parties.	
Papot	16/6/16		Usual Training Programme. Preparations for 10 days relief. Gas attack at 12.10 am. No Casual [—] No very little gas came over	
PLOEGSTEERT	17/6/16	10.5am	Relieved 11th R.W.K. in Ploeg St trenches T121, 122 & 123 Relief complete 4.5am. On our left 26 R.F. On our right 21 K.R.R. Quiet both day and night.	
— do —	18/6/16		Everything normal during the day. Usual working parties detailed by 122nd Brigade	
— do —	19/6/16		12.5 am. Gas alarm. No gas noticed. Quiet sunday day. 5 pm. Smoke bombs thrown from T123 by Bombers. Enemy retaliated [—] rifles had very little damage. Usual working parties.	
— do —	20/6/16		Everything normal	
— do —	21/6/16		— do — Trenches 121, 122 [—]	

Army Form C. 2118.

WAR DIARY
or
INTELLIGENCE SUMMARY
(Erase heading not required.)

Instructions regarding War Diaries and Intelligence Summaries are contained in F. S. Regs., Part II. and the Staff Manual respectively. Title Pages will be prepared in manuscript.

Place	Date	Hour	Summary of Events and Information	Remarks and references to Appendices
PLOEGSTEERT	22/6/16		Day quiet and uneventful. 11.30 pm. Gas alarm sounded on our left: Heavy Artillery bombardment - our Artillery much superior to that of Enemys. No noticeable explosions in S1 and S2.	
— do —	23/6/16		Very quiet morning and. Several working parties. Between 9pm and 9.30 pm. enemy continued shelling the road and made three bursts at the Strand. Shells fell up near B&D Gladeshe House, Rolelmi attacked from our Artillery. Enemys fire soon down by ours. A party from Trench much damaged side.	
PAPOT	24/6/16		Relieved by 11th R.W.K. Relief complete 8.50 am. Casualties during week - killed 1 NCO & 2 men, wounded 5 NCO's & 4 men - including 3 NCO's wounded by defective rifle grenade. Battalion inspected by C.O.	
— do —	25/6/16		Working parties and Church Parade. Major Monifen left to command 18th K.R.R. Major Clarke commanding "B" Coy took over from him.	
— do —	26/6/16		Usual working parties. Company training when Company arrangements.	
— do —	27/6/16		Usual working parties. Rifle inspected by Armourer Staff Sergeant.	
— do —	28/6/16		Usual working parties	
— do —	29/6/16		Visited by Sir John Bethell M.P. Presented medals to Batt. Football team.	
— do —	30/6/16		Usual working parties. Casualties for week 1 NCO wounded on working party. Ashley H. Col Commanding 32 and L.F.s	

46/ July
32. R. Fus
Vol 3
17/4/17

3a

32nd (S) Bn. The Royal Fusiliers

War Diary

July 1916

Army Form C. 2118.

WAR DIARY
or
INTELLIGENCE SUMMARY
(Erase heading not required.)

Instructions regarding War Diaries and Intelligence Summaries are contained in F. S. Regs., Part II. and the Staff Manual respectively. Title Pages will be prepared in manuscript.

Place	Date	Hour	Summary of Events and Information	Remarks and references to Appendices
PAPOT	30/6/16		Usual working parties. Casualties for week 1 NCO wounded on working party.	
PLOEGSTEERT	1/7/16	5 am	Relieved 11th R.W.K. Relief completed 7.10 am. T.121. 122. 123 occupied. New B.H.Q. Lowshow Lodge. Disposition in Trenches altered. B & D Coy as before but C Coy replaced by A Coy - C Coy going into reserve.	
— do —	2/7/16		Rifle Grenades freely exchanged. 2/Lt. Garratt seriously wounded in the leg by enemy rifle grenade at 9.30 am. Died at 5 pm from No 2. Artillery activity normal. Usual working parties. HOSPITAL BAILLEUL	
— do —	3/7/16		Trench Mortars used by B Coy from 26 th R.T. Bahn now occupies T121/4 inclusive. Enemy Trench Mortars active - considerable damage to our front line. Usual working parties.	
— do —	4/7/16		Baths H.Q. moved to Hope House - H.Q. of 26th R.T. Bahn became our offensive unit went arrangements being - two units of 124 Bde relieve the other two units of the same Brigade. Enemy Trench Mortars still very active.	
— do —	5/7/16	11.30 pm	Considerable activity with Trench Mortars on both sides. Our Artillery bombarded the enemy for about an hour. Enemy's retaliation great. Usual working parties.	
— do —	6/7/16		Normal during morning. Our Artillery very active all the afternoon. Enemy Mortars apart from this his reply was tame.	

Army Form C. 2118.

WAR DIARY
or
INTELLIGENCE SUMMARY

(Erase heading not required.)

Instructions regarding War Diaries and Intelligence Summaries are contained in F. S. Regs., Part II. and the Staff Manual respectively. Title Pages will be prepared in manuscript.

Place	Date	Hour	Summary of Events and Information	Remarks and references to Appendices
PLOEGSTEERT	7/7/16		During the day at intervals our Artillery and Trench Mortar Battery bombarded enemy's front line, cutting wire in several places in preparation for a raid by 30 of our men on nte 9th. Our machine guns active during the night - preventing enemy repairing his wire. Retaliation feeble.	
— do —	8/7/16		——— do ———	
— do —	9/7/16		Quiet during the day. Raid. Copy of Report attached. 10.30 p.m. During the night considerable Rifle and machine gun fire on both sides.	
— do —	10/7/16		Uneventful day. Usual working parties. Casualties for the Tour - 1 Killed - Wounded 4 H.W.Wells - 2711 Noble (wounded) and 11 O.R.	
CRESLOW	11/7/16		Relieved by 26th R.F. Relief completed 8 am	
— do —	12/7/16		Usual working parties	
— do —	13/7/16		Bathing parade Working parties as usual	

2449 Wt. W14957/M90 750,000 1/16 J.B.C. & A. Forms/C.2118/12.

Army Form C. 2118.

WAR DIARY
or
INTELLIGENCE SUMMARY
(Erase heading not required.)

Instructions regarding War Diaries and Intelligence Summaries are contained in F. S. Regs., Part II. and the Staff Manual respectively. Title Pages will be prepared in manuscript.

Place	Date	Hour	Summary of Events and Information	Remarks and references to Appendices
CRESLOW	14/4/16		Working parties as usual.	
— do —	15/4/16		— do —	
— do —	16/4/16		Church services. 9 am Roman Catholics. 3.30 pm Nonconformists — 7 pm Church of England. 9.30 pm over 10 pm — Ten minutes intense bombardment by our Artillery. Enemy replied vigorously. One of their shells making a have immediately behind Battn H.Q. occupied by Bomb: Signallers — killing one N.C.O. and wounding 1 N.C.O. and 3 others.	
PLOEGSTEERT	17/4/16	6 am	Relieve 26th R.F. Relief completed 7.15 am. Apart from desultory firing — day quiet.	
— do —	18/4/16		Working parties as usual. Everything normal.	
— do —	19/4/16		— do — 27th Inrham — Rw.s — Bringing over Jameson reporter for our own for the on Essengths.	
— do —	20/4/16		— do — Went Patrol on Uttrecht bring round to our position Reserve	
— do —	21/4/16		— do —	

WAR DIARY or INTELLIGENCE SUMMARY

(Erase heading not required.)

Army Form C. 2118.

Place	Date	Hour	Summary of Events and Information	Remarks and references to Appendices
PLOEGSTEERT	22/7/16		Uneventful day. Usual working parties. Patrol from B Coy brought in an old Minenwerfer shell from Machine Gun House. 2/Lt Rishel reported for duty to 122 I.B. T.M.B.	
PAPOT	23/7/16 5.30 am		Relieved by 26th R.F. Relief complete by 9 am. 11.30 am Nieuweyngenouds Service. 6.30 pm Cpl C. C. Enterby reported for enlargement. Casualties for week.	
— do —	24/7/16	6.30 am	Medical inspection of "A" Coy. 6 pm Kit Inspection of D Coy by C.O. Bathing parades at NIEPPE. Usual working parties.	
— do —	25/7/16	6.30 am	Medical Inspection of "B" Coy. 10 am Adjutant's inspection of H.Q. Coy. 6 pm C.O's Kit inspection of C Coy. Bathing parades at NIEPPE. Usual working parties.	
— do —	26/7/16	6.30 am 3 pm 10 am 11 pm	M.O's inspection of C Coy. Kit inspection of B Coy. Bathing parades. Lecture to Officers by C.O. 2/Lt Carey reported for duty on strength of Batn. Gas alarm sounded. All ranks stood to with Gas Helmets on. Heavy bombardment by our Artillery. 11 pm no gas came over. Res Muck. 2/H Carey reported for duty and Inkerman taken on strength.	
— do —	27/7/16	6.30 am 3 pm	M.O's inspection of D Coy. 2/Lt Benjamin returned to duty. Kit inspection of B Coy 2/Lts Skinner, Hainault and Bayard reported for duty. No change. Bathing parades at NIEPPE. Casualties 4/L Killed H.O. Latham wounded	4/13 O.R.

2449 Wt. W14957/M90 750,000 1/16 J.B.C. & A. Forms/C.2118/12.

Army Form C. 2118.

WAR DIARY
or
INTELLIGENCE SUMMARY
(Erase heading not required.)

Instructions regarding War Diaries and Intelligence Summaries are contained in F. S. Regs., Part II. and the Staff Manual respectively. Title Pages will be prepared in manuscript.

Place	Date	Hour	Summary of Events and Information	Remarks and references to Appendices
PLOEGSTEERT	28/7/16		1 am Gas alarm sounded + no gas noticed at Papot. 5 am Relieved 26 R.F. - took old original lines, T.M.I. 172 - 17.3. B C Coy relieving B Coy into reserve. 9/4 July reported for duty and taken on strength Everything normal	
do	29/7/16		Everything normal. Usual sniping parties.	
do	30/7/16		— do — do —	
do	31/7/16		Two Court Martials — one held at Bn HQ Plouarch House on Pte Owen, charged with failing to appear when warned for duty in the trenches. Copy inside. The other held at Papot on Sgt Ramsey, charged with being drunk and in prohibited area without a pass. Everything normal.	

P.M. Gyle
L. Gyle
Commanding 32nd Royal Fus.

C/338

TRENCH RAID.

A party consisting of 30 N.C.Os & men of 32nd R.F., under 2nd Lt Wills left T 123 at 10.30 pm and arrived at enemy's wire at approximately place fixed at 11.30 pm.

The wire was 24 ft thick and had been cut satisfactorily, but was badly tangled. The party got through easily and the cutting had been well carried out

Immediately the battery opened fire, 2nd Lt Wills jumped over the enemy's parapet.

The trench was about 5'6" deep by 3 feet at top and 2 feet at bottom, duck boarded and in splendid condition. He landed practically on a machine gun behind which was an apparent dug out.

He was closely followed by L/Cpl Swann and Cpl Maynard who helped him pick up gun and throw over parapet preparatory to bringing back. The cartridge belt got entagled in barbed wire and the gun had to be left in a shell hole near the parapet, as the trio were being badly bombed and could not receive support from rest of party on this account.

Whilst this was being done, an officer emerged from the dug out previously mentioned and shot 2nd Lt Wills through the shoulder with a revolver. 2nd Lt Wills shot him through the head.

Afterwards throwing a bomb down the dug out to prevent further attackers coming out.

Another man then came round an angle of the trenches calling CAMERADE.

Being comparatively unsupported - as his N.C.Os were struggling with the guns - 2nd Lt Wills was compelled to shoot him.

By this time the enemy's bombs - which were all high explosive - were coming over in great numbers, preventing reinforcements arriving and making further advance impossible.

2nd Lt Wills therefore ordered the party to return immediately and received a slight bullet wound in his right leg.

The arrangements throughout went without a

1. (Back)

hitch.

Our artillery was accurately placed and the mortar holes made as a guide by our T.M.B. were invaluable.

May the previous report about our artillery barrage falling short be cancelled, please?

This was reported by some of the men who had apparently mistaken enemy's bombs for our own shrapnel. And it is not confirmed by Officer in charge of party

Enemy's artillery retaliated at 11.40 pm with about 30 5.9 shells on BUNHILL ROW and over Wood and also shrapnel on front trenches.

The conduct of 2nd Lt Wills appears to have been admirable throughout and he showed great coolness and presence of mind......................
....

I also wish to mention the names of
    Cpl MAYNARD and
    L/Cpl SWANN
who stuck to 2nd Lt Wills throughout...........
....
....

(Signed) R.E.Key,
    Lt Col., Commdg
    32nd Bn Royal Fusiliers.

1.50 am
Night of
9/10th July, 1916.

WAR DIARY or INTELLIGENCE SUMMARY

Army Form C. 2118.

of 7/2nd K.R. Fusiliers Vol U

(Erase heading not required.)

Instructions regarding War Diaries and Intelligence Summaries are contained in F.S. Regs., Part II. and the Staff Manual respectively. Title Pages will be prepared in manuscript.

Place	Date	Hour	Summary of Events and Information	Remarks and references to Appendices
PLOEGSTEERT	1-8-16		Uneventful day. Usual working parties.	BHQ
- do -	2-8-16		Quiet during the day. At 9.43 p.m. fire lit 11.36 p.m. and artillery shelled enemy positions at intervals. Enemy retaliated by replying. Quiet and easy of never - also sending over several Trench mortars on our front line.	BHQ
CRESLOW	3-8-16	5am	Relieved by 11th R.W.K. Relief completed 7.30 am. Moved to CRESLOW from 15th Hants. Branches for the week N°18	BHQ
- do -	4-8-16		Working parties detailed by 122nd BRIGADE. Shed by 5/15 recognition fire from our Artillery by whom the work in 6 of Lines. 1 killed and 13 wounded - 3 of those subsequently died in Hospital	BHQ
- do -	5-8-16		Resting parties. Enemy sent up no our fireworks to 18th KRR who also were very prompt and threw lance and their trains. 6 of our fire were trembled and dangerous Divine.	BHQ
- do -	6-8-16		Glen of Spires. Day of rest unless thought end. The change in commemoration of 2 in Anniversary of outbreak of War. All working parties suspended.	BHQ
- do -	7-8-16		Usual working parties. One man hit whilst on working party.	BHQ

2449 Wt. W14957/M90 750,000 1/16 J.B.C. & A. Forms/C.2118/12.

Army Form C. 2118.

WAR DIARY
or
INTELLIGENCE SUMMARY
(Erase heading not required.)

Instructions regarding War Diaries and Intelligence Summaries are contained in F. S. Regs., Part II. and the Staff Manual respectively. Title Pages will be prepared in manuscript.

Place	Date	Hour	Summary of Events and Information	Remarks and references to Appendices
CRESLOW	8-8-16		Bathing parades at NIEPPE. Usual working parties. Casualties for week 4 killed 11 eleven wounded.	E.H.O
PLOEGSTEERT	9-8-16	5 a.m	Relieved 11th R.W.K. Relief completed 6.15 a.m. Enemy artillery active.	E.H.O
do	10-8-16		Uneventful day. G.O.C. 124 Bde visited trenches. Lieut working parties. L.C.M. Lees at Batts. H.Q. finished forge on Pte J Sykes of this unit. 3 barges sentences no active Service when charges of this nature tried. Sentence 40 days F.P. No 1.	E.H.O
- do -	11-8-16		Uneventful day. Conference of Commanding Officers at 124 Bde H.Q.	E.H.O
- do -	12-8-16		Quiet day. Usual working parties.	E.H.O
- do -	13-8-16		do	E.H.O
- do -	14-8-16		do	E.H.O
- do -	15-8-16		Enemy Artillery more active. A new division is believed to be opposite. A rifle numb. enterprise carried out by D Coy. Three Bangalore torpedoes were fired breaching 3 gaps in a faulty system through the breast work were sent up by 3 mers of Rifle retts. An hostile fault appeared in parapet over which officers engaged in the {2/Lt Edwards 2/Lt. Evans E.H.O obliged to return to our own lines.	

2449 Wt W4957/M90 750,000 1/16 J.B.C & A. Forms/C.2118/12

Army Form C. 2118.

WAR DIARY
or
INTELLIGENCE SUMMARY
(Erase heading not required.)

Instructions regarding War Diaries and Intelligence Summaries are contained in F.S. Regs., Part II. and the Staff Manual respectively. Title Pages will be prepared in manuscript.

Place	Date	Hour	Summary of Events and Information	Remarks and references to Appendices
PLOEGSTEERT	16/8/16		Uneventful day. Officers from Battalion relieving the 32nd R. Fus came in town of inspection	
BRESLOW	19/8/16	5 am	Relieved by 8th Battn Yorks & Lancs. Relief completed by 6.30 am. Casualties for week – 1 killed 6 wounded.	
LACRECHE	19/8/16	9 am	Handed over billets at BRESLOW to 10th West Riding Regt. Marched to LACRECHE. arrived 1 pm	
do	19/8/16	7 am	Battalion route march about 6 miles. Lectures on open warfare under Company arrangements.	
do	20/8/16		Divine Service C of E 3 pm. Noncomformist 3-30 pm. Bathing Parades at BAILLEUL.	
do	21/8/16 7am 5.30 pm		Battalion route march to METEREN about 12 miles. Inspection by G.O.C. 27 Infantry Bde HQ Ras. Bridgewater. Banner. BV. Clarke Luncheon to 8th and 9th Battns Royal Fusiliers	
do	22/8/16 8.30 am		Battalion route march about 6 miles. Lectures under Company arrangements 11am till 4.30 pm	

WAR DIARY
or
INTELLIGENCE SUMMARY
(Erase heading not required.)

Army Form C. 2118.

Place	Date	Hour	Summary of Events and Information	Remarks and references to Appendices
LA CRÈCHE	23/8/16	3.28 pm	Battalion entrained at BAILLEUL WEST STATION at 2-30 pm. Train left 3.28 pm	BHQ
BELLANCOURT	24/8/16 6 pm	Arrived PONTREMY at 1.50 am. Marched to BELLANCOURT arriving 4 am. Inspection of Companys intoire billets at 3 pm by C.O. Lecture of C.O. to Company Commanders.	BHQ
do	25/8/16 9-11	Field of operations at EAUCOURT. Trekking Scouring games in SOMME offensive. Lecture to Company Commanders by Major Clark.	BHQ
do	26/8/16	do - do -	BHQ
do	27/8/16	Divined Services Coy E. 10 am - Nonconformists 11-15 am 2.30-5pm Bathing parades at EAUCOURT in stream running into River SOMME. Sgt F. HILL of C Company drowned. Report sent the Brigade.	BHQ
do	28/8/16	Field operations at EAUCOURT. - do - for 25th & 26th	BHQ
do	29/8/16 9 am	do - do - Manoeuvres watched over enlivened by Divisional Commanders and Brigadiers. Battalion route march over night operations.	BHQ

WAR DIARY
INTELLIGENCE SUMMARY

Army Form C. 2118.

Place	Date	Hour	Summary of Events and Information	Remarks and references to Appendices
BELLANCOURT	30/8/16		Weather conditions prevented outdoor work of any description being carried out. Lecture by Major Black to Junior Officers in Map reading.	840
do	31/8/16	9 am 2 pm	Battalion route march to Ailly Le Haut Clocher. Beyond fighting under C.S.M. Bellew of the Army Gymnastic Staff	840

A.W.Leg. Lt Col
Commdg 32nd Royal Fusiliers

Sheet I.

WAR DIARY
or
INTELLIGENCE SUMMARY
(Erase heading not required.)

Army Form C. 2118

12¾/4 Vol 5

32nd Battn Royal Fusiliers

Place	Date	Hour	Summary of Events and Information	Remarks and references to Appendices
BELLANCOURT	1916 1st Sept.		Rain prevented Battn training. Coy afternoon Coy Organization Transport Inspection by O.C. 41st Divisional Train	
IN BILLETS		10.45 AM		W
(4 miles S. E. of ABBEVILLE)	2nd "	8.45 AM 8 PM	Wood Fighting & Battn Training. Night Operations	W
	3rd "	11 AM 3.30	Divine Service. Coy of Enquiry to enquire into death of Sergt F. HILL "C" Coy by drowning 27/8/16/pm. Battn Parade in PONTREMY Camp. (Finding accidentally drowned)	W
	4th "		Rain prevented Battn Training. Coy Organization instituted	W
	5th "		Route March Coy Organization etc	W
	6th "	9 AM 2-6 15 AM	Bayonet fighting Route March to ABBEVILLE Bathing parade at Battns. Battn marched to LONGPRES LES CORPS SAINTS	W
	7th "	7 AM 11 AM 12.30	Battn entrained and went to above Detrained at MERICOURT. Battn marched to Bivouac Camp near EDGE HILL STH TRICOURT.	W

5a

Sheet 2.

WAR DIARY
INTELLIGENCE SUMMARY

32nd Bn Royal Marines

Army Form C. 2118

Place	Date	Hour	Summary of Events and Information	Remarks and references to Appendices
FRICOURT EDGE HILL 8th Bn CAMP	1916 8th 9th AM	9-4.30 AM PM	Presence of Bn Guard dispatched under 2nd Lt DAVIES. (40 O.R.) Coy Training under Coy arrangement. Draft of 77 O.R. arrived from Base.	M
(Map Ref Sh62d)	9th "	9 "	Coy Training. Bayonet fighting. Bomb & Gas Instruction. Lecture on attack at C.O.'s subject met to bivouac near DELVILLE WOOD to report ground & effects of 2nd Lt F.B. WILSON arrived from Base. He returned on duty from Lovett Bates meet to contest FRICOURT	M
FRICOURT (F.M.W. Map)	10th "	10 AM 10-30 AM	Divine Service under Brigade arrangements C.O.'s subject returned having been punished by mud & wheel & was fine from obtaining much information about ground	M
Sheet 62d	11th "	9-12 10 a.m.	Physical Drill. Bayonet fighting. Gas Lecture & drill. Extending Tool drill Lecture on "Gas Precautions." C.S.M. 2nd Bn PAITH FULL M.M. C.Gs - complied with quick & combative defg." Battery parade at VIVIER MILL	M
—	12th "	9-12	Battalion Training	M
—	"	2.30 6 pm	Officers Mess Meeting Check organised for Brigade by 32nd R.M.	M
—	13th "	9-12 3-30 pm	Coy Training Battn moved to camp near N.Z. Divn at FRICOURT.	M
—	14th "	9-12 5 pm	Coy Training & Organisation R.M.E. moved to trenches near Delville Wood, via MONTAUBAN.	M
—	15th "	3.45 am	Battn arrived in position of readily for attack Supporting 10th Queens. Report on action attached.	M
—	16th "		About 160 reorganised & established new Sentel Trench in the South Montl Trench	M

Sheet 3

Army Form C. 2118

WAR DIARY
INTELLIGENCE SUMMARY

32ⁿᵈ Bgⁿ. Royal Fusiliers

(Erase heading not required.)

Instructions regarding War Diaries and Intelligence Summaries are contained in F.S. Regs., Part II. and the Staff Manual respectively. Title Pages will be prepared in manuscript.

Place	Date	Hour	Summary of Events and Information	Remarks and references to Appendices
IN TRENCHES	1916 17ᵗʰ Sept		Remainder of Battⁿ remained in the Support Trench etc. Major W.C. Clarke & Capt. S.S. Smith relieved C.O. & Adjutant Gaidner & G.O.C. letter sent to Transport Camp to report Remainder of day occupied by Burying fatigues.	M
New EDGEHILL Sᵗⁿ. Camp	18ᵗʰ "	7 pm	Battⁿ relieved & proceeded to POMMIER REDOUBT. Battⁿ returned to Transport Lines near EDGEHILL Sᵗⁿ. §32 → 190. 66. Casualties 10 Officers. 289 O.R. Killed Wounded Missing	986
(D.19.d.) Map Sheet (62D)	19ᵗʰ "		Camp struck & retitched on dry ground. Rain prevented Training. Belt Reorganised etc.	M
" "	20ᵗʰ "	12 noon	Inspection of 124ᵗʰ Inf Brigade by G.O.C. in new of Camp. G.O.C. congratulated Brigade on successful efforts on 15ᵗʰ, 16ᵗʰ & 17ᵗʰ inst. Telegram sent in by H.M. the King thro' G.O.C. D La Corps Commander etc	M
" "	21ˢᵗ "	9–12.30 2.00	Battⁿ Training Camp Area C.O.'s Inspection.	M
" "	22ⁿᵈ "		—— do ——	M
" "	23ʳᵈ "	9-12.30 3 pm	Battⁿ = Training C.O.'s Adjⁱˢ Conference at Brigade H.Q.	M
" "	24ᵗʰ "	11 am	Divine Service Battalion Parade at VIVIER MILL.	M

1875 Wt. W563/826 1,000,000 4/15 J.B.C. & A. A.D.S.S./Forms/C. 2118.

Sheet 4.

WAR DIARY
INTELLIGENCE SUMMARY

Army Form C. 2118

3/2rd Bn. Royal Fusiliers.

Place	Date	Hour	Summary of Events and Information	Remarks and references to Appendices
EDGE HILL CAMP	1916 Sept 25	9-12 2.30 2.30	Batt= Training in Camp Area. Attack Practice. Camp attack in medium for men, who did not return for C.O.'s Inspection. Camp Pitched open afts. Inspection.	M.
" (Camp)	26"	9-12 2.50 6 pm	C/o Training in Camp Area. Rehabilitation of trenches from 5 guns (1pm /bg) Batt= Practice. Attack Practice. C.S.M. Graham returned from Base in 22448 Pte FAITHFUL M.W. accompanied to 36 days F.P. No2. first	M. M.
"	27"	9-12 2.50	C/o Training Batt= Parade. Attack Practice. Inter Company Competitions. G.O.C. attended "D" Co supplied winning squad.	M.
"	28"	9-11.30 11.30 11.45 2.45	C/o Training in Camp Area. Attack practice. Putting Parade at VIVIER MILL G.O.C's 174 INF BRIGADE Inspection. Turn out fairly satisfactory. Approved by G.O.C.	M.
"	29"	9-12.30 11 am 2.30 pm	Heavy rain interfered with C/o Training. Lectures to N.C.O's. Batt= Parade. B Co's Inspection. C/o Drill etc.	M.
"	30"	9.30 10.30 2.30	Physical Drill in Camp Area. Attack Practice. Kit Inspection by C.O.	M.

Max. Strength during month. Officers O. Ranks
                              35   984
Min.   "   "   "   26   699
Present "   "   "   28   704

E Ward Lt. Colonel,
Comms 3/2 Bn 15/1/25.
Royal Fusiliers.

SECRET   C O P Y

OPERATION ORDERS

14th Sept 1916.

Reference Maps.
57 C S.W. 1/20,000
Trench Maps (Already issued)

1. **INFORMATION.** The 4th Army in co-operation with the Reserve Army and the French is to attack and capture the enemy's system of Defences up to and including the line MORVAL, - LES-BOEUFS - GUEUDECOURT - HIGH WOOD.
   The Attack will be pushed home with the utmost vigour all along the line until the most distant objectives have been reached.

   1st Objective. The enemy's trenches 800 yds South of FLERS, SWITCH LINE. No halt will be made in TEA SUPPORT TRENCH.

   2nd Objective. Enemy's trenches running S.E. on the S.W. and S side of FLERS, which is known as the FLERS LINE.

   3rd Objective. The Village of FLERS and the line cross roads N.31.B.4.0, Junction Road and N 31.A.2.5.

   4th Objective. Establish line
   N 20.D. 5.0. exclusive,
   N 20.C. 3.6
   N 25.B. 0.6. road junction.
   Track exclusive.
   Where the objective consists of a double line of trenches then assaulting troops will push on and capture the farthest trench.

2. **INTENTION.** The G.O.C intends to attack in four stages on a two Battalion front, two Battalions in front line, 2 Battalions in Support.

3. **DISTRIBUTION.**

1st Line.	10th Bn "Queen's",	right,
	21st K.R.R.C.	left.
Support.	32nd Bn R.Fus.	right.
	26th Bn R.Fus	left.

   Four Vickers' Guns will be attached to 32nd Bn R.Fus.
   Half Section 237th Field Coy. R.E. will be attached to 32nd R Fus to assist in construction and consolidating of Strong Points.

4. **METHOD OF ATTACK.** The Battalion will attack in 4 waves of small columns at not more than 50 yds between Waves. The 1st Wave following not more than 50 yds behind the last Wave of the 10th Queens.

DISTRIBUTION OF WAVES.
1st Wave.

Commdr
Lieut R.GUTHRIE.   Nos 5, 1, 13 & 9 Platoons in the order
                             named, reading from right to left
2nd Lt C.A.HULL,   (R 4 Vickers Guns will accompany this
" " F.A.CAREY,   Wave).

2nd Wave.

Commdr
Capt H.A.ROBINSON   Nos 6. 2, 14, 10 Platoons, in order
2nd Lt J.B.JAMESON,   named reading from right to left.
" " C.W.LANGLEY.   1.   (Back)

CONTINUATION.   (3rd)

                        3rd Wave.
Commdr   Nos 7.3, 15, 11 Platoons in order
Capt W.W.SMITH,   named reading from right to left.
2nd Lt L.C.NICOLL.
 "   " A.W.CLAPTON.
                        4th Wave.

Commdr
Capt A.J.S.BROWN   Nos 8.4.16,12 Platoons, in order
                        named, reading from right to left.
2nd Lt A.L.BENJAMIN.
 "   " S.W.SKINNER.

The 4th Wave will garrison SWITCH TRENCH from COCOA LANE (exclusive) to CADDY LANE (inclusive) and will open up CADDY LANE and connect it with FLARE LANE (the most Northerly point of DELVILLE WOOD,) (Unless this work is done by a Pioneer Battalion.)

When the Artillery barrage rests on an objective, and the Advance is held up Advantage must be taken of all available cover.

5. ASSEMBLY. The Battalion will be in its position of Assembly by 11 pm on the 14th.
   Place of Assembly. Nos 1 & 2 Waves. On right of 26th R.Fs in GREEN TRENCH, 1 wave behind the other.

              Nos 3 & 4 Waves. Immediately to right of 26th R.Fus in EDGE TRENCH, one wave behind then other.
The right of the Battalion will rest on COCOA LANE exclusive
Positions of Assembly & Avenues of Approach will be taped or marked by 10th Queens.
124th Infantry Brigade will be clear of Area S. of YORK TRENCH by 9 pm.

6. AVENUE OF APPROACH. for 124th Infantry Brigade is FLARE LANE.

7. DIVIDING LINES
   (a) between 124th Inf Bde & left Brigade of 14th Div will be the line at Point S 22.C 9.2. and S 17. d 9.8. thence COCOA LANE to its junction with SWITCH LINE.
       T.1 D 8.2.   (Inclus to 14th Div). Road junction
       T 1.B.1.3   (inclus to 14th Div)   "   "
       N.31 B 4.0. (inclus to 41st Div)   "   "
       N 31 B 5.2   (inclus to 41st Div) Strong Point.
       N 26 C 4.4   (inclus to 14th Div) Road Junction.
       N 26 A 9 1   (inclus to 14th Div)
       All houses & gardens at GUEUDECOURT inclusive to 14th Div.
   (b) Dividing Line between Battalions of 124th Infy Bde is marked on your plan. FLARE LANE is the only C.T. to be used by 124th Inf Bde.

8. DIRECTING FLANK. General direction of Attack 28° true bearing. The left Bde will direct.

9. ARTILLERY. The Artillery will form a creeping barrage, troops moving immediately behind it.

10 HOUR OF ASSAULT. At zero hour the leading waves of Infantry will assault. As each wave moves forward its place will be

CONTINUATION.   3.

    taken by the troops in rear, and so on backwards

11. **TANKS.** 10 tanks will co-operate in the Attack and will precede the Infantry, their role is to clear the way for Infantry. The Infantry must follow behind the Tanks (unless the Tanks break down) and should any Strong Point hold up the Infantry they will call for a Tank to assist them by giving the signal 'Enemy in sight' with a rifle.

    The following signals will be used from Tanks to Infantry

        Red flag   = 'Out of action'.
        Green "   = 'Am on Objective'.
    By night, a series of Ts (on lamp) = Out of Action.
        A series of Hs = Am on Objective.

12. **CONSOLIDATION.** Each objective will be consolidated as soon as possible after its capture and made secure against Counter Attack.

13. **CARRYING PARTIES.** O.C. 1st Wave will detail 12 men per Vickers Gun attached as ammunition carriers.
    O.C. 4th Wave will detail 10 men per Stokes Gun attached (20 men in all) as ammunition carriers.
    All men not detailed for special work will carry four extra bandoliers of S.A.A.

14. **STRONG POINTS.** A Strong Point S.P.1 will be constructed and garrisoned by 25 men under 2nd Lt C.W.LANGLEY at T 7 A.2.6.
    A Strong Point S.P.2 will be constructed and garrisoned by 2nd Lt L.C.NICOLL & 25 men at T 1 C 9½ 2½.
    A Strong Point S.P.3 will be constructed and garrisoned by 2nd Lt F.A.CAREY & 25 men at N 31.B 5.3.
    The R.E. will assist in the construction of these Strong Points

15. **LEWIS GUNS.** 2 Lewis Guns will accompany each Wave, but one of these Lewis Guns which accompanies the 2nd Wave will occupy S.P 1 at T 7 A.2.6. and be under the command of 2nd Lt LANGLEY The Wave Commander will be responsible for detailing this gun.

16. **VICKERS GUNS.** Of the Vickers guns accompanying the 1st Wave one will garrison S.P.2 at T 1 C 9½ 2½ and one will garrison S P 3 at N 31 B 5.3.
    If Vickers guns are not available, Lewis Guns will be detailed. O.C 1st Wave is responsible for this.
    As soon as these Strong Points have been constructed and garrisoned the troops occupying the first two German trenches will reorganise and be ready to advance when ordered.
    Lewis & Vickers guns not already detailed for holding Strong Points must push well forward and hold tactical points.

17. **BOMBS.** Every man will carry two Mills Bombs which are to be looked upon as a reserve for the use of Bombing Squads. They will not be thrown but collected and dumped in each successive line gained.

18. **BOMBERS.** Battalion bombers will accompany first wave and be under the 1st Wave Commander's orders.

19. **COMMUNICATION WITH AEROPLANES.** Every Officer & N.C.O and 50 men per Wave will carry two red flares. These are to be lighted in the front line only at intervals of 20 yds on gaining the line of each objective as soon as the contact

CONTINUATION. 4.

aeroplane appears or calls for flares on the KLAXON horn, and again at 2 pm and 5 pm on 15th and at 7 am on 16th September.
Vigilant mirrors are to be attached to the backs of the coats of a proportion of the men.

20. VISUAL AND RUNNERS. The Signalling Officer will endeavour to establish communication both by cable and by visual signalling as the Attack progresses. He will establish a Visual Station at S 6 D 9.3. Runners will be freely used and relay posts have been arranged at intervals of 300 yards in FLARE LANE. Posts will be marked with yellow flags.
Runners should be directed to the top of FLARE LANE and be instructed to return to the Front Line when the message has been delivered to the First Relay Post. 4 runners from B.H.Q will be left at Brigade H.Q. Forward Runner Posts will consist of three men dug in and marked by a yellow flag.

21. PIGEONS. Each Battalion in frontn line will be provided with two pigeons.

22. MEDICAL. Advanced Dressing Station at the Quarry S 22 C 2.6 Aid Post near B.H.Q.

23. PRISONERS OF WAR. Wave Commanders are responsible for making their own arrangements for escorting prisoners back to B.H.Q. An escort of 10% is sufficient.

24. DRAWING OF EQUIPMENT. Units will draw S.A.A, Stokes Ammunition, Bombs, Flares, Rockets and other articles ordered to be carried from their Brigade Dump ontheir way to position of Assembly.
Each Wave Commander will detail the necessary number of men for this purpose.

25. DOCUMENTS. No maps or documents giving informationn of British Trenches must be taken over the parapet.

26. WATCHES. Watches will be synchronised on 14th instant at 10.45 am and 4.45 pm and on 15th at 5 am.

27. RATIONS. Three days rations will be carried and water bottles filled.

28. BATTALION HEADQUARTERS. Battalion Headquarters will probably be in GREEN TRENCH at the commencement of Operations.

14th September, 1916.
Dictated to
all Officers at 12.55 pm.

(Sgd) R.E.KEY,
Lt Col., Comndg
'PEPPER' Battalion.

AFTER ORDER.

29. SIGNALLERS. Four signallers will go with each wave, the remainder to be with Headquarters.

30. SNIPERS. 25% will accompany each wave.

Instructions have previously been given as to equipment to be carried.

C O P Y.

From   O.C. 32nd (S) Bn Royal Fusiliers.

To   H.Q., 124th Infantry Brigade.

The attached Reports of the ACTIONS on 15th, 16th & 17th September, 1916, are forwarded for information, please, in accordance with Section 139. F.S.R. Pt II.

(Signed) R.E.KEY.

Lt Colonel,
Commdg 32nd (S) Bn R.Fus.

20th Sept., 1916.
ENCS.

SUMMARY of REPORTS.

1.   REPORT by O.C. 32nd Bn Royal Fusiliers,

2.   REPORT by Intelligence Officer, 32nd Bn Royal Fusiliers.

3.   REPORT by Lewis Gun Officer,

4.   REPORT from 2nd Lt L.A.M.DUNLEA, Battalion Signalling Officer.

5.   REPORT from Capt A.J.S.BROWN, Officer Commanding 4th Wave.

6.   REPORT from 2nd Lt C.W.LANGLEY, surviving Officer of 2nd Wave.

7.   REPORT from 2nd Lt J.B.JAMESON, surviving Officer of 2nd Wave.

---------oOo---------

Reference Maps.

57 C. S.W. 1/20,000.
Trench Maps.

C O P Y.

REPORT on OPERATIONS
on 15th, 16th & 17th September, 1916,
carried out by 124th Infantry Brigade
near FLERS.

OPERATION REPORT No 1
by
O.C. 32nd (S) Bn Royal Fusiliers.

At 6.20 am on 15th September, 1916, the 32nd Bn Royal Fusiliers advanced from position in Support to the 10th Bn the "Queen's" 200 yds in advance of DELVILLE WOOD.-

1. DISPOSITION. 26th Royal Fusiliers supporting 21st K.R.R.C, being on our left flank, and 14th Div on our right flank.

2. BARRAGE. Our barrage opened punctually and was extremely effective. The Battalion followed close to the barrage and were able to reach the first two lines of German trenches, viz., TEA SUPPORT TRENCH and SWITCH TRENCH, the resistance being comparatively weak, the enemy having evidently suffered severely from our previous bombardment. The enemy's barrage opened in reply almostb immediately across NO MAN'S LAND, and consisted genereally of H.E. Thisnwas subsequently lifted on to the Wood which was searched systematically and again at intervals during the day, fire on the front edge and left flankn of the Wood being particularly effective.

3. ADVANCE. The Battalion originally advanced in four waves in support, after the first two trenches were reached and the 4th Wave remained behind to consolidate, the other three waves became mixed up with the survivors of the 10th "Queen's", men of the 26th R.Fus, whoh had lost direction and also some of the 14th Division. When SWITCH TRENCH had been won, the remnants of the waves which advanced consisted of two parties -

 (a) under Captain H.A.ROBINSON,
 (b) under Lieut W.V.ASTON,
both being about 80 strong.

A. The former pushed on with his party beyond FLERS capturing three field guns, 5 Officers and about 40 other ranks. The field guns were subsequently destroyed by the enemy's concentrated artillery fire. Prisoners were sent to the Corps Cage, but were apparently taken to the 14th Division in error.

B. The secondn party occupied a position near SUNKEN ROAD, and owing to M.G. fire and sniping from the far end of FLERS were held up until a tank advanced from SUNKEN ROAD and silenced enemy fire. The party then advanced beyond FLERS and dug in under heavy shrapnel fire. Lieut W.V.

CONTINUATION.   (2)

ASTON was later ordered by a superior officer to withdraw his party owing to lack of Supports, and further advance from SUNKEN ROAD was not made until the afternoon of the 15th when this party again advanced beyond FLERS until held up by M.G. fire.

4. **CASUALTIES.** When the Battalion was eventually withdrawn, figures were as follows :-

	Killed	Wounded	Missing	Total
Officers	Nil	10	Nil	10.
Other ranks	28	168	87.	283.

5. **COMMUNICATION.** Full details are forwarded under the Battalion Signalling Officer's Report attached. Communication was very difficult throughout.
   Very heavy shelling caused the transfer of Battalion Headquarters three times, and casualties amongst runners who knew the way being very great, considerable difficulty was experienced in communicating with the Front Line until lines were successfully laid and kept in working order.
   Communication with the Artillery was absolutely impossible but the presence of an F.O O at B.H.Q would probably have simplified matters.

6. **MEDICAL ARRANGEMENTS.** The Regimental Medical arrangements were satisfactory throughout, the Battalion Stretcher Bearers doing especially good work, but no R.A.M.C stretcher bearers or Relay Posts were available. This considerably delayed the evacuation of the wounded, and, in many cases, led to wounded men being killed before they could be removed, the work being too heavy for the regimental stretcher bearers to cope with unaided.

7. **PRISONERS.** 5 Officers and about 77 other ranks were captured by this Unit. The majority were of a poor type and appeared dazed. Several stated that they had only recently come into the line and in most cases about 2 days and that they had suffered very severely from our artillery. Others mentioned that their own feeding arrangements were quite satisfactory.
   They were apparently not greatly affected by the appearance of the Tanks, and it is suggested that they had in all probability been warned of their existence either through spies or through the noise made by the Tanks in approaching.

8. **TANKS.** Apparently the Tanks were considerably impeded by the unsuitable nature of the ground. In spite of natural difficulties, however, they appear to have done very good work, one in FLERS Village and another near GUEUDECOURT causing heavy casualties.
   Captain H.A.ROBINSON, of this Unit, on his way to the Field Dressing Station stated that he saw a tank near GUEUDECOURT put a field gun out of Action before it was subsequently put out of action by another gun of the same Battery.
   In one case the smoke from a tank's exhaust caused considerable confusion amongst a party of the enemy whom it came upon rather suddenly. It is stated that they imagined the smoke to be a new form of gas and endeavoured to adjust their gas helmets before hurriedly retiring.

2.

CONTINUATION.

9. **Strong Points.** Two Strong Points were constructed by this Unit -
    (a)   at   T 1 C 9½ 2½.
    (b)   at   T 7 A 2 6.

These were immediately observed by the enemy's artillery, and were, in both cases, destroyed almost at once. Although persistent efforts were made to rebuild them, the heavy shell fire made this impossible.

10. **ARTILLERY.**
    (a) <u>British</u>. Our Artillery fire on the 124th Inf Bde Sector of the Line was most successful. Large numbers of German dead were found in most of the German trenches occupied, and 25 bodies were taken from a small portion of SWITCH TRENCH alone The shooting on FLERS and GUEUDECOURT appeared particularly accurate.
    (b) <u>Enemy's</u>. During the earlier stages of the Action on the 15th instant the enemy's artillery was very ably handled and undoubtedly caused the greater majority of our casualties throughout. In view of the rapidity with which all targets were fired upon, it is obvious that the enemy's O.Ps were very favourably situated. Even the smallest parties moving between DELVILLE WOOD, FLERS and GUEUDECOURT were fired upon, and in some cases a single stretcher party was considered worth firing upon. The Field Guns advancing down FLERS ROAD were also fired upon very quickly and accurately immediately they came into sight over the top of DELVILLE Wood ridge.
    No chemical shells of any sort were noticed by or reported to this Unit, but several prisoners complained of having suffered from our chemical shells.

11. **COUNTER ATTACK.** Only two ineffective counter attacks by Infantry have been reported by Officers of this Unit and this appeared to have been nipped in the bud by our Artillery fire.
    At about 6.15 pm a very heavy bombardment of all the captured positions and also the edge of DELVILLE WOOD was commenced, but it was not followed up by the enemy's Infantry.

=================oOo=================

16th & 17th September, 1916.

On the above dates this Battalion did not participate in any active fighting, but remained in reserve in positions captured.
    Apart from the heavy artillery fire which was experienced almost incessantly during these two days, there is nothing to report.

                                           (Sgd)   R.E.KEY,
                                                     Lt Colonel,
20th September, 1916.   Commdg 32nd Bn R.Fus.

THE FOLLOWING POINTS WERE BROUGHT TO NOTICE DURING THE ACTION", AND ARE SUBMITTED AS SUGGESTED FOR THE CONSIDERATION OF THE G.O.C.

1. It is suggested that more attention should be paid to preliminary organisation and also reconnaisance.

2. A large number of unnecessary stores etc were carried into the Attack. It is suggested that rations, water and ammunition are really only absolutely essential and that stores etc could be sent up by carrying parties after dark.

3. It is essential that all Regimental Aid Posts should be placed in sheltered positions well behind the Support Line.

4. Stretcher bearer Relay Posts should be established between Front Lines and Support Lines and Regimental Aid Posts and from thence to the Dressing Station.

5. Trench mortars did not appear to be particularly suitable for the Attack although every effort was made by the T.MB Officers to keep them in Action. Two parties were sent from this Unit at great risk and duly arrived but the ammunition was unprotected on arrival and was immediately blown up.

6. It appears advisable that proportion of Machine Guns and Lewis Guns should be retained in reserve to be sent up when positions have been consolidated.

7. Better communication with the Artillery seems imperative This was more neglected during the Advance than it was in the trench warfare at PLOEGSTEERT.

8. An increase in the scale of pigeons issued to Battalions is recommended.

9. A long march immediately before the Attack should be avoided.

10. Necessity of ensuring that important messages reach their destination. One most important one was never delivered, and the Officer concerned only heard of it through another Unit.

11. Supports should be very close and easily get-at-able.

Army Form C. 2118.

WAR DIARY
or
INTELLIGENCE SUMMARY
(Erase heading not required.)

Sheet 1.

32nd (S) Bn: Royal Fusiliers

Place	Date	Hour	Summary of Events and Information	Remarks and references to Appendices
Near EDGEHILL STN. CAMP	1916 Oct. 1st	11 am	Church Parade	Map Ref: Ln. D. D.19 d.
		1 am	WINTER TIME came into use. Two pieces moved back 1 hour.	
		2.30 pm	Conference of Officers.	
		4.30	Washing of clothes at VIVIER MILL.	
		7.0 pm	Training Other Methods.	WE
" "	2nd "	7.30 am	Camp Offices.	F.G.A.
		8.45 am	Battalion Parade. C.O.'s Inspection.	
		1.30 pm	Battalion Paraded, marched to Camp at POMMIERS REDOUBT, arriving 7.15 am	
		9.30 pm	Dinners served.	WE
POMMIERS REDOUBT	3rd "	2 pm	Battalion marched to trenches (support) at SUNKEN ROAD (M35 d.6.5) arriving 9 pm. Major M.C. CLARK commanding & Capt. F.C.B. SMITH as Adjutant.	
Support NR TRENCHES	" "		Under orders to move forward. Capt. F.C.B. Smith wounded about 12 noon by fragment of gun near HE Shrapnel	M.35 d. 8.5
			Capt & Adjt E.T. COOPER arrives at 9.30 pm. Movement Order Cancelled Suspended for 24 hours.	WE
	5th	4.30 pm	Enemy Artillery very active. Day X my LC. Large number for our Battalion. Shrapnel going into R.T. S-9 mostly etc.	A 19 C.62
			Batt= relieved 11th R.W. Sussex. R.H.Q. H.Q. at Factory Corner. Colour fitted company Somme owing with Luvain, fishing, shelling & Packs & what would Luvain, Gulin, Red C.O. & carry to etc, but there were brought by adj. b 2.5ft	
			Factory Corner was shelled incessantly day & night. EDWARDS Sergt	WE

WAR DIARY or INTELLIGENCE SUMMARY

(Erase heading not required.)

32nd (S) Bn Royal Fusiliers.

Army Form C. 2118. Sheet 2.

Place	Date	Hour	Summary of Events and Information	Remarks and references to Appendices
GIRD SUPPORT & ADVANCED TRENCHES	1916 Oct 6th	11.30	Enemy Artillery very active during entire day. Disposition: D.A. + B. Coys in Stop Point Line. "C" Coy in support, B.H.Q. and "A" Coy in front line & occupied at temporary shelters. Whole Batt worked all night in digging new trench which has been done previous night by R.E.'s. Entrenching Party toils completed at daybreak.	No. 19a 4.4. P/L
"	" 7th		New Trench was not occupied as it was found 26th R. Fus had not dug their front to link up with ours. Our Heavy Artillery fired short for first hour, did great damage to our trenches, all front Coy Casualties were attended with some little difficulty by Bn front and shelter were very scarce. Casualties see attached. The Batt relieved at 1.45 p.m. but was marched to Carnoy camps & drafted.	P/L
"	" 8th		Major L.C. CLARK Batt was ordered to Quarries at 10 a.m. 9. L/Cpl R.E. REY in GIRD TRENCH. No. 19b 0.9. took over command. B.H.Q. in shelters in Sunken Road in Somme Front. C.O. left to attend Conference at B.H.Q. at 3 p.m. Our shepherd fired intermittently Bn attended Chinese Trench, scarce activity. Our shepherd fired upon heavy fire.	No. 19b 0.9. P/L
"	" 9th		Draft of 3 officers & 19 O.T. arrived. Trench mortar lines. Day was spent in clearing front line. Red Cross flag to wall surrounded. We extended Red Cross flag with aid of red fire for Hn Officers line. Trench all ie hands work completed.	P/L
"	" 10th	9.30 p.m.	Hostile flares very active. Flying over on front support line. New communication trench was dug to front line. Men exhausted. Batt was relieved at 9.30 p.m. by 2nd Royal Scots. Casualties during tour: Officers 11 O.T. 229	11 P/L N.6a.
MAMETZ WOOD CAMP.	" 11th		Batt arrived at MAMETZ WOOD Camp at 5.30 a.m. Proceeding by train to BECORDEL Camp at 10 a.m., arriving 1 a.m. Day spent cleaning up equipment, clothes and reorganising.	N.6a. P/L
BECORDEL CAMP.	" 12th	8.30 10.— 11.—	C.O. organising Battn Parade Kit Inspection. Draft of 1 Officer & 60 O.T. arrived.	E.12 a. P/L

WAR DIARY
INTELLIGENCE SUMMARY
(Erase heading not required.) 32nd (S) Bn Royal Fusiliers

Sheet 3.

Army Form C. 2118.

Instructions regarding War Diaries and Intelligence Summaries are contained in F.S. Regs, Part II. and the Staff Manual respectively. Title Pages will be prepared in manuscript.

Place	Date	Hour	Summary of Events and Information	Remarks and references to Appendices
BECORDEL Camp.	19/16 Oct 13th		2 Drafts of 40 arrived. Capt E.T. COOPER relinquished Adjutancy on promotion to Major. 2nd Lt C.E. EDWARDS took over A/Adjutancy.	M
"	" 14th	9.00 a.m 2.30 p.m	Inspection of Drafts by C.O. Bayonet fighting, Physical Drill etc.	M
BUIRE	" 15	9.15 a.m 2 p.m	Battn marched to BUIRE BILLETS. Draft of 201 arrived. Church Parade Division. Dukelski M.Mulcahy Cmmsnd to Cmpts DALZELL & Pte BARTLETT. Lecture on Planning of Trench Raid by M.O. Statistics Training	M M
"	" 16th		Battn entrained at MERICOURT at 6.30 p.m. Army marched to BUIRE. Draft of 36 men arrived. Tactical Train very uncomfortable & very slow. Mile for line average speed.	M
LONG PRES	" 17th	1.30 p.m	Battn arrived at LONGPRES. Accommodation provided is very good billets. Battn spent remainder of day in cleaning up etc.	M
"	" 18	11 a.m	Battn Parade. Specialist Training continued. Rain prevented work in afternoon.	M
"	" 19	9.30 - 10.30 11.30 - 11 - 12 2 pm	Instruction in Sea Measures, Helmets etc Bayonet fighting. Care & use of Rifle, Bayonet etc. Cleaning up	M
		12.42	Battn entrained for CAESTRE.	

WAR DIARY • Sheet 4

INTELLIGENCE SUMMARY

(Erase heading not required.) 32ⁿᵈ (S) Bⁿ Royal Fusiliers.

Army Form C. 2118.

Place	Date	Hour	Summary of Events and Information	Remarks and references to Appendices
METEREN AREA	1916 Oct 20ᵗʰ	9:30	Returned at CAESTRE, & marched to scattered billets in METEREN area. Draft of 38 O.R. arrived.	
PATRICIA Camp.	" 21ˢᵗ	9 am 12:30 pm	Battⁿ marched to PATRICIA Camp. Arrived at destⁿ. Coy. Orgⁿ. Coⁿ Organised. Coys Guides proceeded to RIDGE WOOD trenches.	PM PM
RIDGEWOOD	" 22ⁿᵈ	7ᵖᵐ 2:15	Battⁿ proceeded to RIDGE WOOD. Support trenches & took over from 4/6 A.H.B. Relief completed.	M.5 & 8.3 PM
	" 23ʳᵈ	9 am 5:30 pm	Battⁿ practised trench routine & relieving in old trenches near retrenchments. Working Party of 200 provided for R.E.s and throughout month.	PM PM
	" 24ᵗʰ	9 am	Coⁿ Organisatⁿ Specialist Training	W
	" 25ᵗʰ	4 am	do C.O. (Lt Col. R.E. Kay) went on leave. Major E.T. COOPER took over command.	PM
	" 26	9 am	Packing Medals etc 1 Officer & 2 O.R. went on leave.	W

353/B3

WAR DIARY or INTELLIGENCE SUMMARY

Army Form C. 2118.

Sheet 5.

(Erase heading not required.) (32nd (s) Bn Royal Fusiliers.

Place	Date	Hour	Summary of Events and Information	Remarks and references to Appendices
RIDGE WOOD HUTS.	1916 Oct 27	9 a.m. 2 p.m.	A, B, C's Billetted at RENINGHELST. C & D. A.Q. C. do	M/
Trenches	" 28	2 p.m.	Batt'n relieved 10th Queens in Trenches. No losses suffered relieving. Enemy shelled sector. Trenches waterlogged.	M M.10 & 77.
"	" 29	9 a.m. 5.45 p.m.	Heavy Rain. no available water supply in Frontline. Div. Commander & Brigadier inspected line. H.Q. Inf. Brigade at 5.45 pm or matter in on in night.	M
"	" 30		Repair of Trenches en continued. Dugouts improved trenches.	M
"	" 31		—— do ——	M

	Officers	Other Ranks.
Maximum Strength during Month.	28	977
Minimum " " "	15	493
Present " " "	25	971

M/
Major,
Kindly Comm'g 32nd Bn
Royal Fusiliers.

WAR DIARY or INTELLIGENCE SUMMARY

Army Form C. 2118.

SHEET 1

32nd (S) Bn ROYAL FUSILIERS

Place	Date	Hour	Summary of Events and Information	Remarks and references to Appendices
VIERSTRAAT	1/11/16		Major W. C. CLARK rejoined from 10th "Queens" and took over Command.	Bn.H.Q. N1062.9
		3pm	Conference of C.O's & Adjutants at Bge Hdqrs.	
			Good Bns views 4th Australian Artillery "shoots" at S.45pm, 6.17pm, 7.14pm, 7.42pm, 8.15pm	
"	2/11/16		Lt. YORKLEW proceeded to BASE to relieve Capt. SOUSSE, M.R.R.W. Kent.	
		10.30am	G.O.C. 41st Division visited the Trenches.	
		4pm	Collection fired near from our art.	
		midn.	Enemy shelled NEW RESERVE TRENCH and artillery N.16.b.10.Tel opposite N17.b.7.7. Patrol sent out from N12.d.3.1 - N18.b.2.8. Relief 2.15 am.	
"	3/11/16	8.45pm	Relieved by 10th Bn "Queens". Relief complete 12.30 am 4-11-16.	
LA CLYTTE	4/11/16		H.R.H. The Duke of Connaught visited H.Q. Divisional area of RENINGHELST. Usual Working Parties supplied.	N7 Central
"	5/11/16	10 a.m.	Baths at LA CLYTTE from 9 am to 4.15 pm. Usual Working Parties. Conference of C.O's at 1pm Inf. Bge. Hdqrs.	
"	6/11/16		Battalion fitted with Small Box Respirators. Usual Working Parties.	

Army Form C. 2118.

WAR DIARY
or
INTELLIGENCE SUMMARY
(Erase heading not required.)

32nd (S) Bn ROYAL FUSILIERS

SHEET 2

Instructions regarding War Diaries and Intelligence Summaries are contained in F.S. Regs., Part II. and the Staff Manual respectively. Title Pages will be prepared in manuscript.

Place	Date	Hour	Summary of Events and Information	Remarks and references to Appendices
LA CLYTTE	7/11/16		C.O. returned from leave. Evening Working Parties cancelled owing to bad weather. Inspection by 2nd Army Commander cancelled.	
- " -	8/11/16	10 am	Conference at B.H.Q. Mess of Officers. Usual Working Parties.	
- " -	9/11/16	2 pm	Relieved 10th Bn "Queens" in Right Sub Sector commencing at 2 pm. Relief complete 5.15.	
VIERSTRAAT	10/11/16		Day & Night Working Parties engaged for Front Line work.	
- " -	11/11/16		Day & Night Working Parties supplied for Front Line work.	
- " -	12/11/16		Inter Company relief. Usual Working Parties for Front Line work.	
- " -	13/11/16		Usual Working Parties for Front Line work.	
- " -	14/11/16		Usual Working Parties for Front Line work.	

Army Form C. 2118.

WAR DIARY
or
INTELLIGENCE SUMMARY

SHEET 3

32nd (S) Bn ROYAL FUSILIERS

(Erase heading not required.)

Instructions regarding War Diaries and Intelligence Summaries are contained in F.S. Regs., Part II. and the Staff Manual respectively. Title Pages will be prepared in manuscript.

Place	Date	Hour	Summary of Events and Information	Remarks and references to Appendices
WIERSTRAAT	15/11/16		Relieved by 10th R. "Queens" commencing at 2 p.m. Relief complete 3.35 pm	
RIDGEWOOD	16/11/16		Usual Working Parties supplied.	NSCebd
" "	17/11/16		3 Officers & 80 O. Ranks to Brigade Bombing School for training for raid. Usual Working Parties supplied.	
" "	18/11/16		Usual Working Parties supplied.	
" "	19/11/16		Usual Working Parties supplied.	
" "	20/11/16		Usual Working Parties supplied.	
" "	21/11/16		Sunray Raid carried out by 39th Inf. Bge. at SPANBROEK MOLEN. Usual Working Parties supplied. Relieved 10th Bn. "Queens" at Right Bn. H.Q. commencing at 4.30 pm. Relief complete 5.15 pm.	

Army Form C. 2118.

WAR DIARY
or
INTELLIGENCE SUMMARY

SHEET 4

32nd (S) Bn ROYAL FUSILIERS

(Erase heading not required.)

Place	Date	Hour	Summary of Events and Information	Remarks and references to Appendices
VIERSTRAAT	22/11/16	10 a.m.	F.G.C.M. at Bn H.Q. on Pte. Saturn, tried & found. Men dismissed. MURRUMBIDGEE CAMP	
			Usual Working Parties for Front Line Work. Enemy Artillery exceptionally quiet.	
-"-	23/11/16		Major E.T. Cooper proceeded to Bde: Bombing School as o/c Raid. Raid fixed for 25th inst: cancelled. Usual Working Parties for Front Line Work.	
-"-	24/11/16		Inter. company relief at 2 p.m. Usual Working Parties for Front Line Work.	
-"-	25/11/16	5.30 p	Lecture on Reading Aeroplane Photograph at Bn: Hdqrs. Usual Working Parties for Front Line Work.	
-"-	26/11/16		Usual Working Parties for Front Line Work.	
-"-	27/11/16	2 p.m.	Relieved by 10th Bn "Queens". Relief complete 3.45 p.m.	

Army Form C. 2118.

WAR DIARY
or
INTELLIGENCE SUMMARY

(Erase heading not required.)

SHEET 5

32nd (S) Bn Royal Fusiliers

Instructions regarding War Diaries and Intelligence Summaries are contained in F. S. Regs., Part II. and the Staff Manual respectively. Title Pages will be prepared in manuscript.

Place	Date	Hour	Summary of Events and Information	Remarks and references to Appendices
LA CLYTTE	8/11/16	9.30 a.m.	Inspection of clothing by Companies.	
		2.0 p.m.	C.O's Inspection by Companies.	
		5.0 p.m.	Conference of Officers at Bn H.Q.	
			No Working Parties supplied by Divisional Commander's order.	
"	29/11/16		Baths at LA CLYTTE allotted from 9 a.m - 4.15 p.m	
			Naval Working Parties supplied.	
"	30/11/16		Naval Working Parties supplied.	

	Officers	Men
Maximum Strength during month	26	975
Minimum " " "	24	966
Present " "	26	966

Ashley Hart Colonel
32nd Bn Royal Fusiliers

Army Form C. 2118.

WAR DIARY
INTELLIGENCE SUMMARY
(Erase heading not required.)

Sheet I.

32nd (S) Bn Royal Fusiliers

Vol 8

Place	Date	Hour	Summary of Events and Information	Remarks and references to Appendices
Vierstraat	1916 Dec 1st	2 pm	Battalion relieved 10th Queen's R.W.S. Regt in Trenches. Relief completed by 3-50 pm. Usual working Parties.	Bn J.H.Q. N.10.6.2.9
"	2nd		RAID carried out on Enemy Trenches by the Battalion. (See attached Report)	
"	3rd		Enemy artillery quiet throughout the day. Our artillery was active during the day. Usual working parties.	
"	4th		Julio Coy Relief. Our Artillery active during the morning. G.O.C. 86th Infy Bde. visited our front line at 10 am.	
"	5th		Lt Col R.E. Key Comdg proceeded to take over Command of 124th Inf Bde during absence of Brig Genl W.T. Glennon on leave. Major W.C. CLARK took over Command of Battn. Enemy artillery more active. B.J.H.Q. Shelled.	
"	6th		VIERSTRAT Shelled by Enemy with H.E. Our artillery shelled Enemy T.M.B. positions.	
RIDGEWOOD	7th		Battalion relieved by 10th Bn Queen's R.W.S. Regt & proceeded to RIDGEWOOD. Relief completed by 6/30 pm.	Bn J.H.Q. N.5 a 7½ 2

WAR DIARY
INTELLIGENCE SUMMARY
(Erase heading not required.)

Army Form C. 2118.

Sheet II.
32nd Bn Royal Fusiliers.

Place	Date	Hour	Summary of Events and Information	Remarks and references to Appendices
RIDGEWOOD	1916 8th Dec		Uneventful day. (Edwards)	By J.K.P. No. 5473a2.
"	9th Dec.		Enemy sent over some "TEAR" Gas Shells on RIDGEWOOD. Enemy aircraft active during the morning. Battalion bathed at REMING HEIST. (Edwards)	
"	10th		41st Siege Artillery carried out a shoot at 2 pm on enemy's chief lines of communication to cause casualties to enemy transport. (Edwards)	
"	11th		124th Inf Bde T.M.B. bombarded enemy lines in front of HOLLANDSCH/SHUUR SALIENT at 2 pm. (Edwards)	
"	12th		RIDGEWOOD shelled by enemy with H.E. & shrapnel during the morning from 10am - 11am. (Edwards)	
VIERSTRAAT	13th		Battalion proceeded to Front Line to relieve 10th Bn Queens U.W.S Regt. Relief completed at 6/30 pm. (Edwards)	By J.K.R. No. 10629
"	14th		Enemy artillery active during the morning. VIERSTRAAT shelled for morning. Left Div'l Artillery carried out shoots on enemy line at 1/8 pm. Enemy about 100 strong raided the 26th R.F. on our left at 7pm. Our Artillery immediately opened fire & the enemy were driven out. Our Lewis Gun fire was very effective. Our Casualties - 1 Officer wounded 4 wounded. (See Copy Report attached) (Edwards)	

WAR DIARY of INTELLIGENCE SUMMARY

Army Form C. 2118.
Sheet III, 32nd Bn. Royal Marines.

Place	Date	Hour	Summary of Events and Information	Remarks and references to Appendices
VIERSTRAAT	1916 Dec. 15th		Enemy Artillery fairly active. VIERSTRAAT shelled during the morning with H.E. & Shrapnel. Expected Raid by Enemy in evening. Edwards	B.M.R. No. 1062.9
"	16th		41st Divnl Artillery carried out Shoot on MARTENS FARM at 1 pm & 3 pm. Draft of 75 o.r. arrived from Base + accommodated in Transport Lines. Capt. W. WATSON rejoined for duty from Base. Enemy's T.M.'s active. Our Artillery active during Aftn. Edwards	O.F.A. 60. No. 1062.9
"	17th		The 41st Divnl Artillery Carried out Shoot at 8 pm & also from 0.30 to 5.0 to 0.84 9.5. Edwards	
"	18th		Our Artillery slightly active. VIERSTRAAT shelled by Enemy during morning & afternoon by T.F. Edwards	
"	19th		Enemy aircraft slightly active.	
LA CLYTTE	20th		Battalion relieved by 10th Queen's R.W.S. Regt at 3/45 pm & proceeded to Regt Billets at LA CLYTTE. Enemy placed several T.M's & Wh.33 Bangs on Bnrt. & Support lines during the morning, doing no damage. Schwartz	No. 7 Central
"	21st		Battalion Bathed at LA CLYTTE Baths. Draft 66 o.r. of Recent draft left POPPERINGHE at 9 am for Musketry Training in II Army School of Musketry at TILQUES. Battalion XMCA Hut at LA CLYTTE by in Concert in evening. Heavy rain during the day & high wind. Brunwin	

Army Form C. 2118.

WAR DIARY
INTELLIGENCE SUMMARY
(Erase heading not required.)

32nd Royal Fusiliers.   Sheet IV

Instructions regarding War Diaries and Intelligence Summaries are contained in F.S. Regs., Part II. and the Staff Manual respectively. Title Pages will be prepared in manuscript.

Place	Date	Hour	Summary of Events and Information.	Remarks and references to Appendices
LA CLYTTE	1916 Dec 22nd		Uneventful day.	N.7 Central
"	23rd		Conference between O/C CO. M.Ss. as to Christmas arrangements. Officers (returned)	
"	24th	11.45	Church Parade. Divn Commander presents Military Medal ribands to Sergt RICHARDSON, L/Cpl G. PACKER, Pte SAMUELS, L/Cpl AMOS, Pte HELMET. During the aft. he spent in decoration of Huts. (returns)	
"	25th		Church Parade in morning. Christmas dinner was served under arrangements & receive from Commander in Chief, Army, Corps, Divn & Brigade Commandt. The day proved to be most successful. (returns)	
"	26th		Lt HILL-LOWE & Sgt WILSON of 8th Cavalry Corps arrive on attachment for instructional work. (returns)	
VIERSTRAAT	27th	5/7.30pm	Battalion proceeds to line in relief of 10th Queen's R.W. Surrey Regt. Relief completed by 7.30 P.m.	(returns) N.10 b.2.9
"	28th		Our Artillery fairly active. Patrol consisting of 2 Officers + 2 O.r. left Nr.12 at 1.15 & 11pm to examine Enemy wire in front of our 2eth, the patrols front line suet. no patrols encountered. aircraft (returns)	
"	29th		Major W.C. CLARK (which proceeded to 41st Brgd TRAINING CAMP as STEEMVOORDE as COMMANDANT on attachmt. MAJOR LOCKHART of 2/4/10 LIVERPOOL REGT arrives for instruction.	
"	30th	1.45pm	Lt Col R.E.KEY proceeds to PARIS on leave. Capt W.Y.ASTON took O/C command of Batt. Lt/Bde T.M.Bs bombard Enemy line & enemy retaliated B.T.Q. being Shelled with H.E. 2 p.m. & damage done to B.T.Q. Sentry at VIERSTRAAT killed by Shell during the morning. (returns)	
"	31st		Enemy artillery active during the morning. POPPY LANE being considerably damaged. (returns)	

Battn Strength officers Off. OR
Drafts wanted 30, 1001 2449
"   recd -   25, 950-
                    20, 1000

Capt Elliott for Capt J. Gee
Adjutant 32nd Rl Fusiliers

Army Form C. 2118.

WAR DIARY or INTELLIGENCE SUMMARY

Sheet I.

22nd (S) Bn: Royal Fusiliers

Place	Date	Hour	Summary of Events and Information	Remarks and references to Appendices
VIERSTRAAT	1916 Dec 1st	2 pm	Battalion relieved 10th Queens R.W.S Regt in Trenches. Relief completed by 3-50pm. Usual working Parties.	Bn HQ N.10.6.2.9
"	2nd		RAID carried out on enemy Trenches by the Battalion (See attached Report)	
"	3rd		Enemy artillery quiet throughout the day. Our artillery was active during the day. Usual working Parties.	
"	4th		Lieut Col Neliel. Our Artillery active during the morning. G.O.C 16th Infy Bde visited our front line at 10 am.	
"	5th		Lt Col R.C. Kay Command to take command of 121st Infy Bde during absence of Brig Genl W.S. Kerman on leave. Major W.E. Clark took command of Battn. Enemy artillery more active. B.J.H.Q. Shelled.	
"	6th		VIERSTRAAT Shelled by Enemy with HE. Our artillery shelled Enemy F.M.B positions.	
RIDGEWOOD	7th		Battalion relieved by 10th A.B.: Queens R No 8 Regt & proceeds to RIDGEWOOD. Relief completed by 6/30 pm.	Bn HQ N.547.2.2

WAR DIARY or INTELLIGENCE SUMMARY

Sheet II.
32nd Bn. Royal Fusiliers.

(Erase heading not required.)

Place	Date	Hour	Summary of Events and Information	Remarks and references to Appendices
RIDGEWOOD	1916 8th Dec.		Uneventful day.	B: H.Q. N. 5.7342.
"	9th Dec.		Enemy sent over some "TEAR" Gas Shells on RIDGEWOOD. Enemy aircraft active during the morning. Battalion bathed at REININGHEIST.	
"	10th		41st Siege Artillery carried out a Shoot at 2 pm on an enemy's chief line of communication to cause casualties in enemy transport.	
"	11th		174th Tr. Bde T.M.B. bombarded enemy line in front of HOLLANDSCHSHUUR SALIENT at 2 pm.	
"	12th		RIDGEWOOD Shelled by enemy with HE + Shrapnel during the morning from 10am - 11 am.	
VIERSTRAAT	13th		Battalion proceeded to front line to relieve 10th Bn. Queen's R to S.Regt. Relief completed at 6/30 pm.	R.X.Q. N. 10.629.
"	14th		Enemy artillery active during the morning. 4.2" Enemy artillery carried out Shoot on VIERSTRAAT Shelter in morning, about 100 shells ranged the 2nd R.M. on our left at 1 & 6 pm. Enemy fire + the enemy were driven out. Our Artillery immediately replied. Our casualties - 1 O.R. killed, 4 wounded. (See copy report attached)	

WAR DIARY or INTELLIGENCE SUMMARY

Army Form C. 2118.

Sheet III
32nd Bn. Royal Munsters

(Erase heading not required.)

Place	Date	Hour	Summary of Events and Information	Remarks and references to Appendices
VIERSTRAAT	1916 Sept 15th		Enemy Artillery fairly active. VIERSTRAAT shelled during the morning with H.E. & Shrapnel. Suspected raid by Enemy in evening.	No. 7652
	16th		4 A/F Brit Artillery co-operated and shot on MARTENS FARM at 1 pm & 3 pm. Battery of 75 or arrived from base & accommodated in Transport lines. Capt MYTH rejoined for duty from base. Our Artillery active during aft. Enemy's T.M.s active during aft. No. 112 Brit. Artillery carried out shoot at 8 pm on road from 0.30.5.0 & 0.8d.9.5.	0 & 6.0
"	17th			
"	18th		Our Artillery slightly active. VIERSTRAAT shelled & Enemy during morning afternoon by H.E.	
"	19th		Enemy artillery slightly active.	
LACLYTTE	20th		Battalion relieved by 10th Queens R.W.S Regt. at 3/45 pm proceeded to Rest at LA CLYTTE. Enemy placed recent T.M. & Whizz Bangs on Bns Regt support N.7 Outre lines during the morning. Day no casualties	
"	21st		Battalion Bathed at LA CLYTTE Baths. Recent 66 or 4 Recent drafts left PEPPERHAMS at 9 am for MUSKETRY training as 14th Army School of Musketry at TILQUESSE and proceeded by Car & Bn. Concentrated XXX Cnr Hut as LA CLYTTE by in Evening	N.7 Outre

WAR DIARY or INTELLIGENCE SUMMARY

Army Form C. 2118.

Sheet IV
32nd Royal Fusiliers.

Place	Date	Hour	Summary of Events and Information	Remarks and references to Appendices
LA CLYTTE	1916 Dec 22nd		Uneventful day.	N.7 Central
"	23rd		Conference between OC & 2/Lt O.C. M.S. as to Christmas arrangements.	
"	24th		Church Parade. Divl Commander presented Military Medal ribbands to Serg RICHARDSON, L/Cpl G PRYER Pte SAMUELS, L/Cpl AMOS. N/Lt In Withers Drill. OC left to attend to details of Xmas.	
"	25th		Church Parade in morning. Christmas dinner was served water by Arrangements from Coy Commanders in Chief Army Corps. OC Brigade Comdg Sgt OC The day proved to be most successful.	
"	26th		1st Hull LONG & Sgt HIGSON of 8th B Cavalry Corps arrived on attachment for instructional work.	
VIERSTRAAT	27th		Battalion proceeded to line in relief of 10th Queens Rl's Surrey Regt. Relief completed at 5pm march via our winter route. Patrol Cemetery of 2 Officers + 29 or left N Post 10:45 Returned 11pm Patrol under Enemy wire in front of our posts. Reported front line field between.	R+J+R N10 6 29
"	28th		Major 2/E CLARK (late B Trench) proceeds to 11th Bn TRAINING CAMPAS STE ANNEXEd to CONTAINED MAJOR LOCKHART of 21/100 MINEURS OR REST arrived No/B relieved	
"	29th		L/Cpl ROKEY proceeds to PARIS on leave. Cpt W V ASTON took over command of Bn. 4:45pm Pte J Rose Pte W McA conducted Enemy Trench enemy works at 2 Sap. being from artillery action during the morning. MM Crate being considerable damage.	
"	30th		Shells with 2 Coy + 7 M.R. Battery at VIERSTRAAT killed 2 SAP during the morning. MM Crate being considerable damage.	
"	31st		Nil O.R.	

Capt & Lieut Col Comdg 32nd R.F.

REPORT OF LT. COL. R. E. KEY ON THE RAID
CARRIED OUT ON NIGHT 2/3rd DECEMBER 1916.

NARRATIVE. At 10 pm the raiding party, consisting of 4 Officers
10 pm   and about 90 N.C.Os and men, arrived in busses at
        B.H.Q. They had previously been fully equipped at the
        Bombing School and no time was lost in marching them
        down to the front line which was reached about 11.10 pm.
        Hot soup being served in POPPY LANE en route. As O.C.
11.10 pm Operations, I established my Headquarters in a dugout
        about 50 yards to the right of POPPY LANE where I was in
        communication with the Brigade H.Q. and Battn H.Q.
        and arrangements were made to establish communication with
        O.C. Raid as soon as his party went over.
11.50 pm At 11.50 pm the raiders began to file out into NO MANS LAND,
        and were able to form up within 40 yards of the enemy's
        wire without molestation. A few very lights were fired
        from the German trenches, but it was remarkable how well
        the party escaped observation, and the absence of M.G.
        fire was especially noticable.
12.5 am Within a half minute of schedule time, the Batteries
12.35 am opened fire, and at 12.35 am (Zero hour) the raiding
        party's signal reel, which had been placed in my dugout
        and was connected to the telephone of O.C. Raid began
        to unwind and so indicate that the party was moving
        forward under the shrapnel barrage. I should here
        like to say that all Officers expressed great admiration
        for the admirable shooting of the Artillery, and it was
        undoubtedly due to their splendid co-operation so few
        casualties occurred.
12.35 am At 12.35 am the first message was received from the
        O.C. Raid to the effect that he was moving forward
        and this had already been surmised by the unwinding of
        the signal drum.
12.41 am At 12.41 am two further messages came through to the
        effect that the enemy's trenches had been successfully
        entered and that several prisoners had been taken. I
        should like to emphasize the value of the forward line
        which kept me in touch with the raiders. The line was
        easily maintained and no difficulty was experienced in
        picking up messages even during the artillery bombardment.
12.53 am At 12.53 am the rockets which were the prearranged
12.55 am signal for return were fired and at 12.55 am the raiders
        commenced to leave the enemy's trenches. O.C. Raid
        (Major Cooper) 2nd Lt. TROTTER, and several slightly
        wounded men reported at my Headquarters shortly afterwards,
        the remainder returning direct to B.H.Q. with the
        prisoners and trophies they had taken.
        2nd Lt. TROTTER, a young Officer whom I wish to
        bring to your notice, Sir, reported to me that he
        believed one of our men, Pte CARRUTHERS, was lying
        wounded in the German trenches and he volunteered to
        go back to search if he could find a few volunteers
        to accompany him.   This I agreed to, and 2nd Lt,
        TROTTER and two men set out to look for the wounded man.
        Major COOPER also volunteered for this work, but I
        would not allow him to go, as I thought one Officer
        sufficient and did not care to risk more than seemed
        more than was absolutely necessary.

Sheet 2.

2nd. Lt. W.P. TROTTER. 2/Lt. TROTTER reached the enemy's parapet but hearing a good deal of shouting and movement in the front line, he decided to return and take out a larger party. I did not agree to this, but it occurred to me, and to the O.C. Raid also mentions it in his report, that after a successful raid a second party of about 30 strong might do considerable damage and take further prisoners when the enemy comes back again to occupy his line.

RETALIATION. The enemy's retaliation was feeble. A few trench mortars of various sizes in the vicinity of POPPY LANE and a sprinkling of whizz-bangs seemed to have been the utmost of his efforts, and less than an hour after the raid I walked back along POPPY LANE without hearing anything except an occasional rifle shot from the opposite trenches.

TRENCHES. The enemy's line appears to be dry and on the right in good, with hurdle revetment. On the left 2/Lt. TROTTER reports that it is not so good, and his impression is that the trenches are shallow and out of repair. L/Cpl COOPER reports that there is no trench round the crater, no signs of an emplacement there, and no wire round or in it. The trench runs behind. Pte SEARs smashed a hosepipe and Lt. DAVIS cut what appeared to be two armoured cables which ran along the trench. There is a diversity of opinion about the wire, but the majority agree that it was little damaged and difficult to negotiate.

SAPPERS. The sappers and tunnellers carried out this work very thoroughly and about 1.15 am the explosion was heard which it is believed destroyed the saphead. Of this I may be able to get further evidence when the Tunnellers are interviewed.

In conclusion I beg to mention that Major COOPer carried out his duties as O.C. Raid entirely to my satisfaction and all the Officers and several men whose names I will submit later seemed to have behaved bravely and helped to make the raid a success.
I believe our casualties to be 2 seriously and 5 slightly wounded, possibly one missing, but I have not yet had an opportunity of having the roll called owing to the men having made their way home.

Major COOPER thinks that about 12 Germans were accounted for, besides the three prisoners, and a few trophies also taken.

Only one man was wounded by retaliation being hit through the calf of the leg by a machine gun bullet.

      I have the honour to be, Sir,
      Your obedient servant,
      (Sd) R. E. KEY, Lt. Col.

6 am 3/12/16.

REPORT ON RAID 2/3rd Dec. 1916.

Sir,

I have the honour to report that the Raiding Party under my command left our trenches at 11.50 pm and lay in NO MANS LAND as close to the shrapnel barrage as possible until 12.30 am when the line advanced in the enemy's front trenches at the two points planned, viz:-

N.18b. 2½.8½ and N.12d.5½.0½.

My party withdrew at 12.50 am. We succeeded in capturing three prisoners, blew up two dugouts known to contain Huns, who resisted and would not surrender, and, it is believed a third, but this is not absolutely confirmed. An enemy's mineshaft or sap was discovered about 20 yards down a communication trench, leading from the centre of their front line, but owing to the darkness and confusion it is impossible to place this more definitely, an exploding charge was placed therein and subsequently exploded.

A sniper's post was also demolished leading out of the sap at "C".

No Machine Guns or emplacements would be discovered. The M.Gs were either withdrawn in the early stages of the bombardment or were in the bombed dugouts.

An enemy's bombing attack on our left flank was repulsed with several casualties, and it is estimated that at least 12 Germans were killed by my party.

OUR ARTILLERY.

The Artillery arrangements throughout, were extremely satisfactory although they apparently opened fire two or three minutes early.

The field artillery did not appear to do much material damage to the front and partially disused trenches in the salient, and it was impossible to verify the damage done by the heavy artillery, but from the bursting of the shells the firing was very accurate and probably accounted for the entire absence of M.G. fire.

ENEMY'S WIRE.

The wire was very slightly affected by the bombardment, but entrance to the trenches was made at the places previously selected.

ENEMY'S ARTILLERY.

The enemy's retaliation was extraordinarily weak, and it is suggested that he may have moved some of his batteries to YPRES quite recently. H.E.

A very ineffectual/shrapnel barrage was attempted across NO MANS LAND but these burst too high to do any considerable damage, and the heavy T.Ms which burst in the customary positions at the head of POPPY LANE did not affect the Raiding Party.

ENEMY'S WIRE.

The enemy's wire was very much thicker and stronger than had been anticipated, in some places it was only three of four coils thick, but in others it ran to a depth of over 30 yards, but was not very high, consisting chiefly of barbed concertina wire.

ENEMY'S TRENCHES.

The Front Line trench was more shallow and narrow than our own, but was in approximately the same condition. Attempts at revetment had been made with hurdles, and the trenches throughout were floored with duckboards.

CASUALTIES.

Our casualties are believed to have been very slight.
One man is reported Missing, but this cannot be definitely confirmed at present.
It is estimated that about 6 men were slightly wounded and one severely. It is believed that there no men killed in the Raiding Party.

ENEMY'S CASUALTIES.

Approximately 12 Huns, who were in the two dugouts blown up, were killed (?)

SUGGESTIONS.

The following points are suggested by experience gained during the raid.

(1) That a raiding party, which is not intended to penetrate to the Support system, should not number more than 50 all ranks.

(2) That the first raid should be followed shortly afterwards by a second bombing attack, and an effort made to take prisoners.

(3) Very experienced and reliable stretcher bearers must be selected for enterprises of this nature.

(4) That the time to be spent in the enemy's trenches might be extended at the descretion of the Raid Commander, if any good results could be obtained.

          I have the honour to be, Sir,
             Your obedient servant,
               (Sd) E. T. COOPER,
                    Major, O.C. RAID.

REPORT ON RAID 2/3rd DECEMBER 1916.

Sir,

I have the honour to report that the whole of the Left Party encountered thick coils of concertina wire, in which there were only two gaps, one a small gap on the left, and one large gap on the right. One half of my party entered by the left gap and one half by the right.

Almost as soon as they entered the trench a dugout was found, and a "P" bomb was thrown in. One prisoner emerged and shouted "Boys, boys", but did not like being taken over the parapet at all.

The Left Flanking Party bombed to "C" meeting with resistance between "B" and "C". A bombing fight ensued in which one of our men was wounded. About 20 bombs were thrown by our men and the enemy retreated. A sniper on the left was also troublesome.

We partially demolished a sniper's post.

The trench itself was very narrow and shallow, having duckboards, but only being revetted at certain parts.

After a quarter-of-an-hour the left party left the trench, finding difficulty in getting through the wire again.

It is feared that the man wounded in the bombing fight may have been left.

      I have the honour to be, Sir,

        Your obedient servant,

         (Sd) W. P. TROTTER,
           2nd Lt. O. i/c Left Party.

3/12/16.

Copy of REPORT by O.C. "D" Coy: on enemy operation on evening of
December 14th-1916.

To:- Adjutant,
         KNUCKLE.

REPORT ON NIGHTS OPERATIONS.

At about 9 o'clock this evening the enemy suddenly opened a very heavy fire with trench mortars, whizz-bangs, machine guns and rifles: he appeared to be putting a box barrage on us as most of the stuff fell behind the trench between the F.L.T and the Support Line. I passed the word to "stand to" and as the fire seemed to increase in intensity I gave the S.O.S. call to the gunners for my left sector, and afterwards to those covering my right. The guns answered very quickly with their first 2 or 3 shells, but seemed to take some time after that to get into their stride, firing at a very slow rate for five minutes or so (This is accounted for by the C.O. ordering slow artillery fire on the enemy frontline before the Coy: Commander called for the SOS)

After that, however, they left nothing to be desired either on the score of quickness, accuracy of aim and rapidity of fire.

Shortly after the SOS call one of my men from the extreme left came and reported to me that at about 9.15 p.m. men from DEW came running down from their line to ours, but returned a little later.

The enemies fire slackended at about 10 p.m. and I sent the O.K. to the Gunners at about 10.5 p.m.

In the middle of the bombardment I observed the enemy send up 3 rockets, which brust into two lights, yellow and green, fanwise.

One of my Corporals states that at the commencement of the bombardment he heard a shunters horn blown in the enemies trenches, similar to that which I reported last night.

(Sgd) J. BRUCE JAMESON 2nd. Lieut:

O.C. "D" Coy:

Dec: 15th 1916. 5 a.m.
    The damage to our trenches was not severe & the total casualties appear to be 5 O.R. The enemy did not enter our trenches at any point.

Army Form C. 2118.

WAR DIARY
or
INTELLIGENCE SUMMARY
(Erase heading not required.)

Instructions regarding War Diaries and Intelligence Summaries are contained in F. S. Regs., Part II. and the Staff Manual respectively. Title Pages will be prepared in manuscript.

Place	Date	Hour	Summary of Events and Information	Remarks and references to Appendices
VIERSTRAAT	1/1/17	3pm 5½pm	B.H.Q shelled at 10am to 11.15am by H.E & 4.2's. Little damage. Brigadier General conference of Battalion Commanders. 16th Bn? on night scout. up S.O.S. rocket. Artillery activity abnormal on both sides.	No 4.29
RIDGE WOOD	2/1/17		Battn relieved by 10th Bn. "Queens" R.W.S Regt. and proceeded to RIDGE WOOD. Artillery activity on both sides.	Nos 7.3.
— " —	3/1/17		Enemy shelled S.E. corner of RIDGE WOOD with H.E & Shrapnel from 9.30 to 11 am. Our artillery retaliated.	
— " —	4/1/17		Enemy shelled RIDGE WOOD with H.E. Shrapnel at frequent intervals during the day. Our artillery retaliated. Lieut: Col: R.E. KEY returned from leave and took over command.	
— " —	5/1/17		Considerable aircraft activity on both sides, together with artillery exchanges. House penetrated and ammt. slightly wounding 2nd/Lt. E.G.S.E.TRENAYNE. 3 men were badly hit. Particular attention was paid to a Pioneer Battalion working on NEWTRENCH. Visibility high. Draft of 66 OR returned from MUSKETRY course at TILQUES	Nos 42.5

2449 Wt. W14957/M90 750,000 1/16 J.B.C. & A. Forms/C.2118/12.

Army Form C. 2118.

WAR DIARY
or
INTELLIGENCE SUMMARY
(Erase heading not required.)

Instructions regarding War Diaries and Intelligence Summaries are contained in F. S. Regs., Part II. and the Staff Manual respectively. Title Pages will be prepared in manuscript.

Place	Date	Hour	Summary of Events and Information	Remarks and references to Appendices
RIDGE WOOD	6/1/17		Our Trench Mortars were very active & carried out a shoot on the enemy's wire at 2.45 pm, supported by artillery. Enemies reply feeble. Baths at LA CLYTTE allotted to Unit all day. Heavy rain in the evening.	
"	7/1/17		During the morning the enemy sent over 600 shells - 4.2 & 5.9 - having apparently located a battery behind RIDGE WOOD. Most of the shells fell in DICKEBUSH LAKE & no damage was inflicted. Enemy aircraft active & one was worried by our machines & A.A. guns & driven off.	
RIDGE WOOD	8/1/17	9 am	Enemy shelled RIDGE WOOD - 3 casualties rec. - Sgt. LEAHY & Cpl. STANYER - KILLED L/Sgt. BURLEY - wounded. Battn. relieved 10th Bn "Queen's" in right sub-sector. Relief complete 5 pm. B.H.Q. had been evacuated owing to "Queen's" coming owing to intense enemy fire. New B.H.Q. (Company) at N11a.5.8.	N11a.5.8
VIERSTRAAT				
"	9/1/17	7pm	X Corps Heavy Artillery bombarded enemy lines. No retaliation. Quiet day.	
"	10/1/17		Quiet day. Work was commenced on preparing Battle Hdqrs. for occupation.	N11C.3.8

Army Form C. 2118.

WAR DIARY
or
INTELLIGENCE SUMMARY

(Erase heading not required.)

Instructions regarding War Diaries and Intelligence Summaries are contained in F. S. Regs., Part II. and the Staff Manual respectively. Title Pages will be prepared in manuscript.

Place	Date	Hour	Summary of Events and Information	Remarks and references to Appendices
VIERSTRAAT.	11/1/17.		Enemy sent a few H.E. on VIERSTRAAT and continued E.R. B.H.Q. 10th Division (on right) raided enemy trench.	
-"-	12/1/17.		Generally Quiet. A few H.E. on Rt. B.H.Q about 5pm.	
-"-	13/1/17.	3pm	Quiet day. Visibility low. G.O.C and Batt. Commanders conference at Bde. H.Qrs.	
VIERSTRAAT / LA CLYTTE	14/1/17		Generally Quiet. Low visibility. Batt. relieved by 10th Bn "Queens". Relief complete by 3pm	
-"-	15/1/17	5pm	Baths allotted to Unit all day. C.O. inspected battalion by companies. C.O.'s lecture to all officers	
-"-	16/1/17		Quiet day.	
-"-	17/1/17		Quiet day	
-"-	18/1/17.		Lt. Williamson, R.A.M.C, left for duty with 13th F.A. Capt. GRIEVESON, R.A.M.C took up duty as M.O.	

WAR DIARY
or
INTELLIGENCE SUMMARY

Army Form C. 2118.

Place	Date	Hour	Summary of Events and Information	Remarks and references to Appendices
LA CLYTTE	19/1/17		Major Clark returned from 9th Bn. Yorks. 6 new officers joined from Base. A.M.S. (Col. RATTRAY) 41st Division, inspected battalion and reported men in good average condition. Guests by "The Stump" at Querin Hall, La Clytte.	AR
LA CLYTTE / VERSTRAAT.	20/1/17		Batt. relieved 16th Bn. "Queens" R.W.S. in Rt. Subsector. Relief complete 3.25pm. Bn. H.Q. moved to Rn. Battn. Hqrs. at N.11.C.3.8.	AR
"	21/1/17		Enemy shelled Bn. H.Q. with 10.5 shrapnel. No damage done. Low visibility.	AR
"	22/1/17		Some aircraft activity on both sides, but otherwise very quiet day. Work of strengthening New Battn. H.Q. continued.	AR
"	23/1/17		Increased aerial activity owing to high visibility. Weather became intensely cold. -25° at night.	AR
"	24/1/17		Continued aerial activity. Good visibility. Artillery quiet on both sides.	AR
"	25/1/17		Enemy aircraft very active and were engaged by our machines and anti-aircraft. Good visibility. Lt. Col. R.E. Key, Knyvet over his command to Major H.C. Clyde and proceeded on Eng. Leave.	AR

WAR DIARY
or
INTELLIGENCE SUMMARY
(Erase heading not required.)

Army Form C. 2118.

Place	Date	Hour	Summary of Events and Information	Remarks and references to Appendices
VIERSTRAAT RIDGEWOOD	26/1/17		Aircraft on both sides very active. Enemy machines crossed our lines but were driven off by our A.A. guns and machines. Enemy artillery quiet. Cold weather continues. Battn. relieved by 10th Bn "Queen's" R.W.S. Relief complete 4.30pm. Casualties during the day - Nil.	
" "	27/1/17		Our artillery bombarded enemy trenches North of the Bluff for 1½ hours. Enemy's artillery quiet. Kaiser's birthday. Weather intensely cold. 10° at night.	
" "	28/1/17		Bn Hd at RENINGHELST allotted Himalaya to the men to bathe. Artillery on both sides quiet.	
" "	29/1/17		Considerable aircraft activity on both sides owing to good visibility. Artillery quiet.	
" "	30/1/17		Quiet day.	
" "	31/1/17		Slight enemy artillery activity. Our Trench Mortars carried out shoot on enemy trenches, supported by artillery at 2.30pm - 3.30pm. Low visibility.	

Army Form C. 2118.

WAR DIARY
or
INTELLIGENCE SUMMARY

(Erase heading not required.)

Instructions regarding War Diaries and Intelligence Summaries are contained in F. S. Regs., Part II. and the Staff Manual respectively. Title Pages will be prepared in manuscript.

Place	Date	Hour	Summary of Events and Information	Remarks and references to Appendices

	Officers	O.RANKS
PRESENT STRENGTH	36	993.
MINIMUM STRENGTH DURING MONTH	28	993
MAXIMUM " " "	36	1001.

B C Cook.
Major Commanding,
3rd (S) Bn. Royal Fusiliers.

WAR DIARY
INTELLIGENCE SUMMARY

32nd Battn Royal Fusiliers

Sheet 1

Place	Date	Hour	Summary of Events and Information	Remarks and references to Appendices
In the Line VIERSTRAAT	1917 1st Feby	12 noon	The Battalion relieved 18th Bn "Queens" Royal West Surrey Regt in the line at VIERSTRAAT. Relief completed at 12 noon. During the relief Enemy aeroplanes crossed our lines but were driven back by our anti-aircraft guns.	N 10 & 3, 4
"	2nd		Weather cold & frosty. Enemy artillery active. Several H.E. shells bursting over RIDGEWOOD. Our trench mortars showed considerable activity.	"
"	3rd		Weather cold & frosty. Enemy artillery quiet during the morning. Enemy trench mortars retaliated in the afternoon for our T.M. shoot the previous day. Enemy aircraft also active.	"
"	4th		Weather cold & frosty. Enemy artillery active, considerable number of shells sent over Rifle F Wood. A little activity by enemy aircraft, effectively dealt with by our aircraft fire.	"
LA CLYTTE	5th		Weather cold & frosty. The Battalion was relieved by 10th & 13th Bn "Queens" R.W. Surrey Regt in the line & proceeded to LA CLYTTE in Brigade Reserve. Relief completed by 4 p.m.	N 7 & 3, 6
"	6th		Weather cold & frosty. The medical officer inspected the Battalion. Baths at LA CLYTTE allotted to Battn. all day. Lecture by C/O to all officers.	"
"	7th		Weather continues cold & frosty. Day occupied by working parties & Coy organisation.	"
"	8th		Both Coys allotted to Battalion. The Medical Officer lectures to all officers. Weather cold & frosty. ⇄ Usual working parties provided. Preliminary musketry training carried out.	"
"	9th		Cold & frost continues. Battalion went on a Route march of 6 miles. Coy Drum firing practised on range of 134th Inf Bde during the afternoon.	"
VIERSTRAAT	10th		Weather continues cold & frosty. The Battalion relieves 10th Bn "Queens" R.W. Surrey Regt in the line, relief being completed at 3.30 p.m.	N 10 & 3, 4
"	11th		Cold & frosty. Our artillery bombarded Bois GRAND BOIS to which the enemy did not reply. Enemy wire cut by our T.Ms. during the afternoon.	"

Army Form C. 2118.

WAR DIARY
of
INTELLIGENCE SUMMARY
(Erase heading not required.)

Sheet II

32nd B. Royal Fusiliers.

Instructions regarding War Diaries and Intelligence Summaries are contained in F.S. Regs., Part II. and the Staff Manual respectively. Title Pages will be prepared in manuscript.

Place	Date	Hour	Summary of Events and Information	Remarks and references to Appendices
VIERSTRAAT. HOLLANDSCHESCHUUR SALIENT.	1917 Feb 12th		Weather cold & frosty. Our artillery shewed considerable activity throughout the day, but the enemy's artillery remained quiet & inactive. Our T.M's again cut the enemy's wire opposite in front of	N.10 of 3.4
"	13th		Weather cold but thaw commenced. Our artillery active at different times of the day. Enemy artillery not retaliate. Our T.M's cut enemy's wire during the afternoon. A little activity by enemy aircraft.	"
"	14th		Our artillery again active intermittently throughout the day. No retaliation from the enemy. Enemy wire again cut by our T.M's during the afternoon. Aircraft inactive.	"
"	15th		Considerable action during the afternoon. Enemy planes crossed our lines but was driven back by our anti-aircraft guns. Weather cold & frosty.	"
"	16th		Our Stokes mortar cut enemy wire during the day. A patrol went out at 10p.m. to examine result of wire cutting. C.S.M HILL, one of the patrol, was wounded in front of enemy wire. The enemy came in from support to the enemy lines, by 2nd L'ER HOME & one 2nd EL.T.M. The enemy called and two attempts to pin dis-ene him, by 2nd L'ER HOME & one 2nd EL.T.M. Wire did not after fit to be sufficiently cut by the T.Ms.	"
RIDGE WOOD	17th 10		Weather dry. Battalion relieved in the line by the 18th Bn King's Royal Rifle Corps & proceeded to RIDGE WOOD in support. Considerable activity by aircraft on both sides during the day. Casualties 10p. to 16.2.17 &c.	N 5 a 3.87
"	17th		Weather dull. Conference with Coy Commanders held by Capn on general organization of Coys. Enemy artillery active during the day.	"
"	18th		Court of Enquiry assembled at B.HQ at 10am to enquire into loss of a bicycle. M.O. inspects the Baths & lectures the Stretcher Bearers. Usual T.M. wire cutting. Weather dull.	"
"	19th		Our artillery active throughout the day. Enemy retaliation negligible. Our T.M's were active during the afternoon. Weather dull.	"
"	20th		T.M's again engaged in cutting enemy's wire in front of HOLLANDSCHESCHUUR SALIENT during the day. Visibility poor.	"
"	21st		Usual wire cutting by our Trench Mortars. Weather dull. Uneventful day.	"

Army Form C. 2118.

Sheet III

WAR DIARY
INTELLIGENCE SUMMARY
(Erase heading not required.)

3/2nd Royal Fusiliers

Instructions regarding War Diaries and Intelligence Summaries are contained in F. S. Regs., Part II. and the Staff Manual respectively. Title Pages will be prepared in manuscript.

Place	Date	Hour	Summary of Events and Information	Remarks and references to Appendices
VIERSTRAAT	1917 May 22		Weather dull. Battalion relieved 18th Bn Kings Royal Rifle Corps in the line today, the relief Completed at 1-30 hrs. Bn Artillery vehicles on account of relief 2/Lt G.W.CAMPION joined for duty from the Base Depot & posted to "C" Coy.	No 10 & 3 st
"	23		Weather very dull. Bn Artillery (Lewis Guns) at different periods throughout the day in preparation of raid.	"
"	24		Weather dull. Front normal. During the night Raymond the railway halts at 10th Bn Queens Regt opposite LACLYTTE, & their position in the front line. Our Battalion holding the morning RITROHANTE & NEW RESERVE TRENCH in front Carriers in the Vine. Our Artillery galhard during the night against the enemy's defences opposite our Brigade Sector. 16 T.M.Bs Co-operating. See Special Report on this attack.	"
"	25th		Weather dull & overcast. Inter-Coy relief in front line "D" Coy being relieved by "C" Coy. Our artillery quiet throughout the day. Enemy shewed no signs of activity.	"
"	26th		Weather bright & clean with good visibility. At 7.30 am to the West of what seems to be enemy H.Q.'s Superior two shells at B.H.Q. It was apparently a mine in the WYTSCHAETE-VIERSTRAAT Road. At night a party went out to examine but could find no trace of it. Our aeroplanes active in the day.	"
"	27th		Weather bright in the forenoon becoming dull in the afternoon, our artillery Shelled GRAND Bois at enemy's front line at 3 periods during the night. 2/Lt A.P.G. VIVIEN joined for duty posted into "D" Coy. Capt H.A. ROBINSON D.S.O. rejoined from the Base. Raiding party wounded by enemy counter-attack on 15/5/16.	"
"	28th		Weather clear & fine. At 9.50 am Enemy sent up about 30 white light flare between his front and GRAND Bois. Nothing happened as the result of this. The Battalion was relieved by the 10th Queens in the line at 3pm & proceeds to LACLYTTE	N.Y.43.6
LACLYTTE			in Brigade Reserve.	

		Off	Other Ranks
MAXIMUM STRENGTH during month		36	967
MINIMUM STRENGTH " "		34	910
PRESENT " "		38	942

28 - 6 May 1917

Total Casualties during 3 months	K.	W.
	Off O.R.	Off O.R.
	- 4	- 10
	1 Died of Wounds

C.F. Shaunis
Capt & Adjt for Lt. Col Commanding
3/2 Royal Fusiliers

2449 Wt. W14957/M90 750,000 1/16 J.B.C. & A. Forms/C.2118/12.

REPORT OF RAID on HOLLANDSCHESCHUUR SALIENT
By 10th Bn "QUEENS", R.W.S.
24th February, 1917.

At 4.55 pm 24th February 1917 the 10th Bn "Queens" R.WS. successfully raided the HOLLANDSCHESCHUUR SALIENT as far back as the second line i.e. N.18b.24.53 to N.18b.86.93 Many Germans were killed, and 1 Officer and 54 N.C.Os and other ranks have been captured. The majority of the prisoners belonged to the 133rd I.R. (Saxons). Their Officer was a Prussian. Three of them belonged to the 292 Mining Company. The Identifications were normal. A mine shaft sunk from the side of the crater at N.18b.20.80 was successfully blown up and with it some Germans who were concealed in it and refused to come out. The cellars under HOLLANDSCHESCHUUR FARM were found to have been converted into a concrete shell-proof dug-out and after extracting four prisoners from it, it was blown up. Another concrete dugout was blown up on the N.E. side of the SALIENT. The trenches on the N.E. side were found to be in fairly good condition, but those on the W. side were nearly obliterated. Four heavy machine guns were found firmly fixed to concrete emplacements. One was removed and brought back, the other three could not be unfixed and were therefore blown up.

WAR DIARY
INTELLIGENCE SUMMARY

Army Form C. 2118

Sheet N° I

32nd (S) Batn Royal Fusiliers.

Vol XI

Place	Date	Hour	Summary of Events and Information	Remarks and references to Appendices
WIRESTRAAT LA CLYTTE	1917. MARCH 1st		Coy organisation & preliminary musketry in the morning. In the afternoon the Baths were allotted to the Battalion.	N.7. Central. AA
"	2nd		Uneventful day. Weather clear & bright.	AA
"	3rd		The Battalion went on a route march in the morning; an hours halt being given for description of targets, fire control. The Lewis Gun Officer lectured to Officers & N.C.O.'s of Coys. In the afternoon N.C.O's attended at Ranges for firing & instruction in Lewis Gun.	AA
"	4th		Divine service in the morning. The C.O. left to attend a course in Gunnery Officers at WISQUES. Major H.A. ROBINSON, D.S.O. took over command. In the afternoon practise was given at 1st & 2nd. Supervisory training was done.	AA
"	5th		The G.O.C. 124th Infantry Brigade inspected the Battalion on the Parade Ground at 9 am. Weather Col. Wills Drums at intervals throughout the day.	AA
VIERSTRAAT In the Line	6th		The Battalion relieved the 10th Bn. "Queen's" R.W. Surrey Regt in the Right Sub-sector of the line at VIERSTRAAT. The relief being completed at 2 p.m. Enemy Shelled VIERSTRAAT-HALLEBAST ROAD while the relief was taking place.	P.P.Q. N° 10 G.29. AA
"	7th		Weather Frosty. Visibility poor. Our artillery carried out a shoot commencing at 6.30 a.m. on the Enemy's Front line - The Enemy's retaliation was feeble. About 4 of our Enemy Reed over several 4.5 shells which fell about 150 yds. short of Bn. H.Q.	AA
"	8th		Considerable artillery activity on both sides. In the afternoon an attempt was made at Short. Silencing of Enemy Trench Mortars about 4 fell Enemy's artillery Shelled Copse of Crucifix definitely on the right of the VIERSTRAAT-WYTSCHAETE ROAD.	AA

Army Form C. 2118.

WAR DIARY
or
INTELLIGENCE SUMMARY

(Erase heading not required.) 32nd Bn. Royal Fusiliers.

Sheet II.

Instructions regarding War Diaries and Intelligence Summaries are contained in F. S. Regs, Part II. and the Staff Manual respectively. Title Pages will be prepared in manuscript.

Place	Date	Hour	Summary of Events and Information	Remarks and references to Appendices
VIERSTRAAT In the line	1917. MARCH. 9th		The G.O.C. 70th Inf. Bde. visited our sector of trenches in the morning. Between 9.45 - 10.30 am enemy registered on Battery on right of VIERSTRAAT - HALLEBAST Road with about 30 H.E. Shells. This was believed to be in retaliation for the attempt of the Battery between 11-15 - 1 pm the same day to cross our wire, which was unsuccessful. Weather cold & misty.	Bn. H.Q. N.10 b.2.9.
"	10th		The C.O. returned from his Course & resumed Command in the afternoon. Artillery inactive on both sides during the day. It was noticed that the enemy fires all his Very lights from his support line. Weather mild with poor visibility.	MS
"	11th		Artillery quiet on both sides, but there was considerable aircraft activity throughout the day, an aeroplane engaging frequently with the enemy. Weather mild, visibility poor.	MS
"	12th		Battalion relieved by 10th Bn. "Queens" R.W. Surrey Regt., relief being completed by 5.20 pm & proceeded to RIDGEWOOD in Reserve.	MS
RIDGEWOOD	13th		G.O.C. Commanding 41st Div. visited Camp in the morning. C/O and late Conference with all Officers. Weather bright throughout the day.	Nr. S.Eecke
"	14th		Quiet uneventful day. At 10-30 pm the enemy sent over 6 billings - tramp which fell in Ritz H.Q.; no damage. Weather dull & cloudy.	MS
"	15th		Usual working parties. Artillery quiet on both sides.	MS
"	16th		Weather cold & frosty with good visibility. Little artillery activity on both sides.	MS
"	17th		Quiet uneventful day. Artillery quiet on both sides.	MS

WAR DIARY or INTELLIGENCE SUMMARY

Army Form C. 2118.

Sheet III 32nd Bn Royal Fusiliers

Place	Date	Hour	Summary of Events and Information	Remarks and references to Appendices
RIDGEWOOD VIERSTRAAT (In the Line)	Fri MARCH 17th 1916		Weather fine with good visibility. The Battalion relieved the 10th Bn. The "Queens" R.W. Surrey Regt in the line, relief being completed at 8.20am. Artillery quiet on both sides.	N.5 Central No. 10 & 2.9.
"	18th		Weather fine, good visibility. At 9.45am Enemy sent over several H.E. Shrapnel between VIERSTRAAT & RIDGEWOOD. Enemy aircraft active during the afternoon. At 4.10pm an Enemy machine was brought down in case of our Aeroplanes forced to descend behind his own lines.	
"	19th		The G.O.C. 12th Infantry Brigade visits the line. Weather rainy & stormy at intervals.	
"	20th		In the morning officers from 8th Br. GLOUCESTERSHIRE Regt. visited the Baths to acquaint themselves with position & also to learn over from us in the following morning. Snow fell at intervals during the day.	
"	21st		The Battalion was relieved by the 8th Bn. GLOUCESTERSHIRE Regt Commencing at 7am Completed at 8.35am, afterwards assembling at the MINE KRUISE ESTAMINET on the DICKEBUSCH - OYTTEFORD Road. Here 32 motor lorries conveyed the Battalion STEENVOORDE the remaining 2½ miles the journey being about 3 hours. On arriving at STEENVOORDE the Battalion was billeted in the various farmhouses in the vicinity, the town of STEENVOORDE being situated about 1½ miles from B.H.Q.	K 14 b.4.5
STEENVOORDE	22nd			
"	23rd		The morning was occupied by preliminary drill & physical exercises in cleaning up for the inspection in the afternoon. At 3pm the Battalion was inspected by Genl. Sir J.F.C. O PLUMER G.C.M.G. K.C.B. ADC. &c. Commg. the Army accompanied by several Staff Officers. Maj.G.O.C 12th Bde. After the inspection Genl PLUMER took the "MARCH PAST"	fill
"	24th		The day was devoted to training, physical drill & rifle minor musketry, & a lecture drill, for the evening the C/O lectures to all officers. Weather clear & fine day.	
"	26th		Divine Service in the morning followed by a celebration of the Holy Communion. Football all in the afternoon.	

Army Form C. 2118.

WAR DIARY
INTELLIGENCE SUMMARY

Sheet IV
32nd Royal Fusiliers

(Erase heading not required.)

Instructions regarding War Diaries and Intelligence Summaries are contained in F. S. Regs., Part II. and the Staff Manual respectively. Title Pages will be prepared in manuscript.

Place	Date	Hour	Summary of Events and Information	Remarks and references to Appendices
STEENVOORDE	1917 MARCH 26		The Medical Officer inspects the Baths. The Companies carried out Coy & platoon organisation orderly arrangements.	K.14 b.4.c. M.S
"	27		In the morning the Bn. attn. proceeded to a field in proximity to STEENVOORDE for a Gas demonstration to the Gas officer of the 41st Div. which proved all ranks to be thoroughly acquainted with measures to be adopted in case of Gas attack or Gas shell bombardment.	M.S
"	28		Letter was read from the Div'l Commander expressing appreciation of the good work done by the Brigade during the 5 months it held the WYTSCHAETE sector. "A" Coy carried Smokers in the Camp at BEAUVOORDE, whilst here allotted to the Batt'n. the "B" & "D" "B & R" Coys. played Football in the Evening. The final of the Cup was allotted to follow. "C" Coy 32nd "D" "W. & R." Coy v. "B" Coy "WKRs" at B.H.Q. at 10.30 a.m. Coy practices in Coy + Platoon attack formation. Night march cancelled owing to inclemency of the weather.	M.S F.G.C.M. on No.10614 Pte WEBSTER M.S
"	29		Battalion Route march & Outpost Scheme. Dinners in the field. Weather Cold & Showery.	M.S
"	30		The Batt'n carried out march practice attack in preparation for the coming Brigade practice attack. Afternoon Musketry + Football in the Evening. Weather Cold + Showery.	M.S
"	31			

Maximum strength during month   Offrs. O.R.
                                   35   937
Minimum   "   "   "   27   696
Present   "   "   "   39   902

CASUALTIES during the month.

                 Off. O.R.
Killed
Wounded   1   10
Died of Wounds   1   2.

[signature]
Capt. & Adjt.
32nd Royal Fusiliers

WAR DIARY / INTELLIGENCE SUMMARY

Army Form C. 2118.

32nd (S) Bn. The Royal Fusiliers.

Sheet No. 1.

Place	Date	Hour	Summary of Events and Information	Remarks and references to Appendices
STEENWOORDE	1917 April 1st		Divine Service in the morning. The Church of England Service being held in the field at Battalion Head Quarters on account of the celebration of the Holy Communion. In the afternoon sports and football. The Battalion met the 28th Bn. R. Fus. in the Brigade Semi Final. The match being played on the M.G. Coys ground and resulting in a win (2–1) for us. A team of 8 N.C.O.s represented the Battn. in the 3-mile Cross Country race & finished 2nd in the Brigade. Weather cold and wet with snow squalls.	K.I.A. 6.4.8.
"	2nd		A Practice attack was carried out in the morning, the Battalion assembling at the Cross roads at K.8.d.4.2. The Capt. & Staff (Brigade) Commander being present. In the afternoon & evening inter Coy football matches were played.	
"	3rd		During the night snow fell heavily, and in consequence the Practice Brigade Attack had to be postponed until the following day. The time was occupied by Company organisation, lectures and cleaning up.	
"	4th		At 8.40 a.m. the Battn. assembled after Cross Roads at K.8.d.4.2. Proceeded to the grounds for Practice Brigade Attack which was carried out under the direction of the Brigadier. In the afternoon football matches were played between the Coys. The days being dull & cloudy with slight showers at intervals.	
"	5th		Another practice attack was carried out in the morning in accordance with several points which were pointed by the G.O.C. on the previous day's practice. The afternoon was spent at practice at the ranges in the third of the Brigade. Al. ranks dancing in the Division for R.R. Coy. in the third of the Brigade. Football (Cup) Match returned at a distance from the 21st Bn. K.R.R. Coys. (Royal Fusiliers) Result 21st K.R.R. won by 5-3. The Brigade G.M. (Capt. C.G. King R.E.) refereed the match. The day was clear & fine.	
RENINGHELST	6th	10.a.m.	The Battn. formed up outside A Coy. Billets & proceeded to march to RENINGHELST, the Battn. being via STEENVOORDE, ABEELE & BOESCHEPE. On arrival at RENINGHELST at 2 pm the Battn. was accommodated in ONTARIO CAMP. Packs were carried in transport. The weather was bright & sunny.	
RENINGHELST	7th		The day was occupied by cleaning up & Coy. drill & organisation. Football matches were played in the afternoon.	M. 4. 6. 6. 8.

WAR DIARY
or
INTELLIGENCE SUMMARY

(Erase heading not required.)

Army Form C. 2118.

32nd (S) Bn. The Royal Fusiliers.

Sheet No. II

Place	Date	Hour	Summary of Events and Information	Remarks and references to Appendices
RENINGHELST (ONTARIO CAMP)	1917 April 8th		Divine Service was held in the morning, the being Easter Sunday. The day was clear & bright. Football in the afternoon.	Mr. L. L. G.E. High Street 28 Edn.
"	9th		In the morning, Bayonet fighting, Physical Training, Musketry, Platoon drill were carried out under Company arrangement. The C/O, the Adjt & Coy Commanders went up to the line in the afternoon to the right sector of the ST ELOI SECTOR	"
"	10th		Training was carried out under Coy arrangement as the following Bayonet fighting, Physical Training, Sir Pelliot's Box Respirator Drill, Musketry, Lewis Gun & Bombing Instruction + Platoon Drill. Weather sunny + bright. Wind & dust storms at times.	"
"	11th		The same training instruction was carried out today as yesterday. The R.S.M. at RENINGHELST was allotted to the Bn for the whole day. A Court of Enquiry was held at Bn. H.Q. to Enquire into desertion SK Cpl Philpot account. Weather wet & cold.	"
RENINGHELST & LEFT SEC. OF ST ELOI SECTOR	12th		The Bn. today relieves the 12th Bn East Surrey Regt in the right sector of the ST ELOI SECTOR. The relief being completed at 2.45pm. The 12th East Surreys gave an escort help in getting the Bn's baggage with the two companies in the reserve. Here two full HQ shelters got very dear but our axillary was considerably more active than his.	No 6 C.9.92 Batty Hqrs BM Map Sheet 281W
"	13th		At 4.15am the enemy Chimneyed C. Block P.M (Sp) "PRE BRASSERIE" a S.I. of building was RAPHS about 200 yds from P.M.Sp) lost. H.E + 4.2's This appeared to be a regular occurrence each morning at the Coy HQ Staff at Bn. H.Q. were to attend barn P.Bn HQ mess. The day was bright + clear although inclined to be cold. Considerable enemy aircraft activity during the morning, over Saran dealing effectively with them.	"
"	14th		About 12 noon a number of shells were sent over by the enemy apparently in the direction of VOORMEZEELE. At 11.20am the enemy again carried out what is apparently intended for a zone shoot near DEAD DOG FARM (Div J.Q's) to the BRASSERIE. Use 77's + 4.2's. 12 Men casualty I Men fell over the left section at our front line. Much during the morning.	"

WAR DIARY or INTELLIGENCE SUMMARY

Army Form C. 2118.

32nd (S) Bn. The Royal Fusiliers.
Sheet No III.

(Erase heading not required.)

Place	Date	Hour	Summary of Events and Information	Remarks and references to Appendices
In the Line St Eloi Sector Left Sector	1917. April 15th		Enemy artillery was active throughout the day. The enemy retaliates with heavy mortars on left Coy Hq's for our artillery shoot at 8 a.m. Trench S.14 being badly damaged. The weather was clear & bright.	See N.6 & 9.95 Bn. J.Sgr.3
"	16th		Enemy aircraft was active at different times of the day. At 2.10 a.m. a heavy explosion was heard behind enemy front line trench, the direction being apparently opposite trench in the Bn. F.L.T. and VOORMEZEELE EXTENSION. There appears to be considerable movement in the enemy line as heard being inspected in the evening. Our artillery was inactive & the road was shelled.	"
"	17th		There was considerable movement on the part of the enemy throughout the day. Little enemy artillery activity. The day was clear & bright.	"
near RENINGHELST CHIPPEWA CAMP	18th		The Batn. was relieved in the line by the 11th Bn. Royal West Kent (Lewisham Road) Left the line completed at 1.50 p.m. Proceeding by way of DICKEBUSCH to CHIPPEWA CAMP about 3 ½ miles N. of RENINGHELST. The day was cool with shells falling at intervals, being very scarce in plenty.	Bn. Or. 35 & 8.2. Bn. Shell 28 S.W.
"	19th		Usual working parties were found. Baths & cleaning up.	Bh
"	20th		A/Capt. A.L. BENJAMIN O/c "B" Coy. left the Battn. in the morning to take up duty at the Base Training Depot. 2/Lt. A.K. DAVIS returned to duty from Hospital [struck through] ...	"
"	21st		In the morning at 10.30 a.m. a Field Parade was held at which the C/O congratulated 2/Lt. A.C. YATES & the men of the patrol of the 18th April on their splendid work & offensive spirit shewn by them in his patrol as which discovered an enemy working party & covering party, killing at least two. Three of the Enemy. Their Commander Major Genl. S.T.B. LAWFORD C.B. also read out ...	"

WAR DIARY or INTELLIGENCE SUMMARY

Army Form C. 2118.

32nd (S) Bn. The Royal Fusiliers.
Sheet N°. IV.

(Erase heading not required.)

Place	Date	Hour	Summary of Events and Information	Remarks and references to Appendices
RENINGHELST. CHIPPEWA CAMP	1917. April 22nd		Divine Service in the morning. Our Enemy aeroplane pass over our camp quite low nearly got but not hit. Baths at the Camp were allotted to us in the morning. A Lecture Board was held at 15. Hdqs. to examine 5ta Clothing. In the evening one of our aeroplanes of the 20th Squadron left Cappellar as pilot descends in our camp owing to engine trouble. The machine flew away the following morning.	Gr. 35 a. & 2. Map Sheet 28 S.W.
"	23rd In the Line St. Eloi Sector N.W Sector		The Battalion proceeded to the line to relieve the 13th Bn. R.W. Kent Regt. the relief being completed at 1-45 a.m. The Enemy artillery was fairly quiet. During the afternoon the Enemy sent several shells over. An enemy aeroplane flew over our lines a long distance away.	N 6. C. 9.92 Map Sheet 28 Br. Stops S.W.
"	24th		The C/O Lt. Col. W.C. CLARK proceeded to England on special leave for 3 weeks. Major H.A. ROBINSON D.S.O took over the Command. Enemy aircraft was somewhat active during the morning. Crossing our lines several times. Enquiry at Army Hdqrs the Enemy Kit Bag himself there with Service cap marks cap with White cover. Weather clear	
"	25th		During the morning rained in the afternoon the Enemy shelled VOORMEZEELE, SCOTTISH WOOD & CAFÉ BELGE. Nothing of importance occurred. Weather clear during morning.	
"	26th		CAFÉ BELGE and DICKEBUSCH were shelled by the Enemy during the day. Several Enemy working parties were observed at different points of the day. Weather clear - Good Observation - Sunny Periods.	
"	27th		Enemy artillery was less active than usual. A few Hvs H.E. Shells fell in the vicinity of MIDDLESEX LANE & FIRE LINE between 7.30 and 8am. A few stray trench mortars junction of 9 & 0. Joseph & Don't Lines trenches during the afternoon. Patrol which went out under 2nd Lt. YATES in Cappara a prisoner of unable, found no sign of any Enemy patrol in this area. Weather clear throughout.	
"	28th		At 10.40am. Enemy artillery with 5.95's one of which unfortunately fell in a Bay hitting Casualties Cullen-shot Sedan schaliets, on the sea from beaten there. A patrol which went out 2nd Lt. YATES to reconnoitre No Mans Land found no sign of any hostile patrol.	

WAR DIARY
INTELLIGENCE SUMMARY

32nd (S) Bn. The Royal Fusiliers

Sheet No. V

Army Form C. 2118.

Place	Date	Hour	Summary of Events and Information	Remarks and references to Appendices
In the Line St Eloi Sector Left Sector	1917 April 29th		Weather Clear Bright weather. There was a little aerial activity on both sides during the day. The G.O.C. visited the Line accompanied by the Brigade Major. Our medium trench mortars again shelled by the artillery again cut the enemy wire, hostile retaliation being on the Brasserie. Otherwise the day was fairly quiet.	N, 6, C, 9, 3. Balc: 11 A 8.2. Map Sheet 28 SW
"	30th		Weather Clear bright weather. The Trench mortars again cut the hostile wire again to lytte artillery, no retaliation coming from the enemy. Very little aircraft activity on either side.	"

STRENGTH

	Offr.	O.R.
Maximum Strength during the month.	40	913
Minimum " " "	38	892
Present " " "	38	892

CASUALTIES during the month.

	Offrs	O.R.
Killed	–	5
Wounded	1	7
Missing	–	–
Died of Wounds	–	1

30th April 1917.

Major Comm'g 32nd (S) Bn. The Royal Fusiliers.

CAPT. & ADJT.

WAR DIARY
INTELLIGENCE SUMMARY

(Erase heading not required.)

Army Form C. 2118

Sheet No. 1 Vol 13

32nd Royal Fusiliers

Place	Date	Hour	Summary of Events and Information	Remarks and references to Appendices
In the Line ST ELOI SECTOR Left Section	1917 MAY 1st		Weather. Clear, bright & warm with good visibility. Enemy again shelled back areas during the day. Enemy aircraft active in the morning. Our artillery retaliated during the afternoon on "R" line. C's Ptn on Sheet 28 for our practice barrage of yesterday.	N.6.C.9.9½. B.V.J.O.87. Map Sheet 28.S.W.
	2nd		An Officer's patrol went out from O.1 D.9.1½.6 to examine wire ruins PICCADILLY FARM. The wire was found to be 12 "fair" & very obstacle & there was much movement in PICCADILLY FARM. This batt'n relieved by the 23rd MIDDLESEX Regt, the relief being completed by 1pm. Proceed to CHIPPEWA "B" Camp.	G.35.9.8.2. Map Sheet 28.S.W.
CHIPPEWA & RENINGHELST	3rd		Weather clear & fine. Battalion vacated CHIPPEWA Camp. Two Coys proceeding to MICMAC CAMP and two to ONTARIO Camp where Batt'n H.Q.rs was also established.	"
ONTARIO & MICMAC CAMPS	4th		The 2 Coys at Ontario Camp, "B" & "D" Coys carried out preliminary musketry & Specialist training. Baths at RENINGHELST were allotted to the Batt'n & "B" & "D" Coys bathed during the day. Board of Enquiry was held by OC during a.m. The Two Coys at MICMAC Camp, "A" & "C" Coys were in write, clothing withdrawn.	M.H.B.6.8. Map Sheet 28.S.W. H.31.B.3.5.
"	5th		Coys at Ontario Camp carried out Physical Training & preliminary musketry. Coy arrangements. The Two Coys at Micmac supplying working parties. The Range at the Brigade Trench Warfare School was sent to by Officers & N.C.Os. Eclere was visited by Officers in the OC of Special R.E. working party on the employment tactics & training of Special R.E. Bat'n.	"
"	6th		Divine Service in the morning at RENINGHELST. The weather was hot throughout the day. A Trial Stores at the QM's Stores was burned today. Football in the afternoon.	"
"	7th		Coys at Ontario Camp — Physical Training — Coy Training. Court of Enquiry was held at the Adjt Stores to enquire into the loss of a Tent & Stores in the fire. A Lecture was given by the Divnl Commander at the Theatre, RENINGHELST at 4pm today to all Officers & N.C.Os in concert parts.	"

13a

WAR DIARY

INTELLIGENCE SUMMARY (Erase heading not required.)

32nd Bn. Royal Fusiliers

Sheet II.

Army Form C. 2118

Place	Date	Hour	Summary of Events and Information	Remarks and references to Appendices
Micmac & Ontario Camps.	1917 May 8th		The two Coys at Ontario Camp relieve the two Coys at Micmac Camp. Cleaning up & Coy organization in the morning. Musketry Special & Training during the afternoon. Board of Survey was held at the Q.M. Store on the Clothing Withdrawn. Chinghing Nettle Boards, Cauvices & Cakes as a substitute for Green Vegetable, with Meat Ration.	M+B.6.8. & H.31.B.3.5.
"	9th		"A" & "C" Coys carried out Physical Training + Musketry ratios for the line. Battn at Remington.1st. were was by "A" + "C" Coys. "B" + "D" Coys Supplying Working Parties. The Brigade Inspected the two Coys in Training at Ontario Camp. The Brigade Commander accompanied by the Brigade Major.	"
"	10th		"A" + "C" Coys carried out Musketry Training in the morning. All ranks who came out with the Battn at the Divine Service Club at Remington.1st. was given by all ranks. Battn went overseas on 4 May,1916. In all about 286 were present. The 2nd Brigade in Celebration of its Canniversary a candidate to be in its afternoon.	"
"	11th		Weather – dull & showery throughout the day. Preliminary Musketry & Physical Training in the morning & afternoon.	"
" & Chippewa "A"	12th		The Battalion moved to Chippewa "A" Camp Today, completing the move by 4pm. Weather fine.	M.6.A.2.7.
Chippewa "A" Camp.	13th		Divine Service in the morning. Battn at Chippewa Camp were allotted to "A","B" + "C" Coys during the afternoon. The Adjutant Capt. C. Edwards proceed to England on Special leave.	M.6.A.2.7.
"	14th		Physical Training Company training was carried out by "B" + "D" Coys. Stretcher Bearers received instruction by the Medical Officer in first aid + carrying.	"

WAR DIARY or INTELLIGENCE SUMMARY

Army Form C. 2118.

Sheet No. III.

52nd Bn Royal Fusiliers.

Place	Date	Hour	Summary of Events and Information	Remarks and references to Appendices
CHIPPEWA CAMP	15th		Physical Training & Company Training by Coys. Kit Inspections & Coy organisation. M.O. lectured to all Stretcher Bearers. Baths from 8am to 3.30 pm.	M.6.A.27.
"	16th		Weather - wet & stormy. Coy Officers ran Physical training from 7am to 8am. M.O. lectured to all Stretcher Bearers. Baths were allotted again during the afternoon. In the evening the Batt. Entertainment Party gave a Concert at the Church Army Hut at CHIPPEWA CAMP.	"
"	17th		The Batt. left CHIPPEWA "A" Camp at 2pm & proceeded by route march via RENINGHELST to ABEELE arriving there about 5pm. Bivouaced at ABEELE for the night. Weather fine & clear. The Co. Lt Col W.C.CLARK returned from leave & joined the Batt. at ABEELE.	"
ABEELE	18th		At 8.30 am today the Batt. marched to ABEELE STATION where it entrained for WATEN. Arrives at WATEN at noon. Marches to HOUTLE a village about 3 miles from the Station. HOUTLE is a pretty village situated among woods, with the River HOUTLE flowing through it. The Batt. was billetted in farmhouses. Batt. Hqrs. at the Mairie at HOUTLE.	L. 33. D. 5. 4.
HOUTLE	19th		The day was occupied by marketry at the 11th Army "A" Range. Very hot throughout the day.	Q.5.C.65.65. Map Sheet 27 A.S.E.
"	20th		Divine Service in the morning in the Jumping web of 26th R Bn. Bathing in the lake near the Brickfields during the afternoon. Weather - Warm, bright & sunny.	"
"	21st		Training per carrie out as usual under Coy organisation:- Physical Training & Bayonet fighting, Special training of each Section in use of its own weapon, Tactical handling of Platoon in attack & defence. Lecture in the afternoon. Weather hot throughout the day.	"

Army Form C. 2118.

WAR DIARY
or
INTELLIGENCE SUMMARY

(Erase heading not required.)

Sheet No. IV

Instructions regarding War Diaries and Intelligence Summaries are contained in F. S. Regs., Part II. and the Staff Manual respectively. Title Pages will be prepared in manuscript. 32nd Royal Fusiliers.

Place	Date	Hour	Summary of Events and Information	Remarks and references to Appendices
HOULLE	May 22nd		The same Training was carried out today as for yesterday. Weather still continues bright & warm.	Q.5.c.6.5.6.5.
"	23rd		Training the same as for 22nd instant.	"
"	24th		The Battalion proceeded to "B" Range for Musketry. Leaving Billets at 6.30 a.m. Breakfast & Dinner were carried on the Range. The following have been notified as deserving of special mention:- Lt. Col. W. E. CLARK, Hon. Capt. & Q.M. A. HIGHAM, Lt. H. DIPPIE, Lt. H.T. HAMMOND, Capt. SCOBIE, No. 8910 Sgt. DAVIES, W.T.	"
"	25th		Battn. carried out training under Coy arrangements. A Lewis Gun Training Ground & Bombing Gun Jumps proceeded to miniature Range for Instruction under I.G. Army Down Gun Instructors. The Adjt. Capt. C. Edwards returned from leave.	"
"	26th		Battn. left Billets at 6.15 a.m. & proceeded to Brigade Training Ground for training. F.G.C.M. was held on No. 13820 Pte. DALTON.	"
"	27th		Divine Service in the morning. The remainder of the day was occupied by bathing, cleaning up.	"
"	28th		The Battn. left Billets at 6.30 a.m. & proceeded to Brigade Training Ground to carry out a practice in Brigade attack. Breakfast & Dinner in the field.	"

WAR DIARY or INTELLIGENCE SUMMARY

Army Form C. 2118.

32" Royal Fusiliers. Sheet No V

Place	Date	Hour	Summary of Events and Information	Remarks and references to Appendices
HOULLE.	1917 May 29th	6.30 am	The Battalion proceeds to Brigade Training ground, leaving billets at 6.30 am for Brigade Practice Attack. Weather fine & sunny.	Q.5.c.65.65.
"	30th		Brigade Practice attack on Brigade Training Ground. Breakfasts & dinners on the field. At 7.30 p.m. the Battalion left HOULLE & marched via WATTEN STATION where it entrained for MOERBEKE at 8.45 p.m. arriving there at 3 a.m. Motor lorries conveys us to RENINGHELST & we arrive at MIDDLE CAMP WEST, South of DICKEBUSCH, at 7.30 a.m.	"
MIDDLE CAMP WEST.	31st		The day was occupied by rest & cleaning up. Supplies drawn for looking parties. In the evening, the Battn. supplied men for looking parties.	N.I.A.0.8

CASUALTIES during May, 1917.

	Offrs.	Other Ranks.
Killed	—	4
Wounded	—	2
Missing	—	nil
Died of Wounds		

STRENGTH during Month.

	Offrs.	Other Ranks.
Maximum	37	944
Minimum	35	875
PRESENT	35	958

Capt. & Adjt.
for Lt Col Commanding
32 Royal Fusiliers

"A" Form.
MESSAGES AND SIGNALS.
Army Form C. 2121.
(In pads of 100.)

TO — H.Q. 124th Inf Bgde

Sender's Number: Y/114.
Day of Month: 5/7/17

Herewith War Diary for June 1917. Please aaa

From: O/C C Bty
Place: BHQ

Capt q ...

WAR DIARY or INTELLIGENCE SUMMARY 2 Royal Irish

Army Form C. 2118.

Place	Date	Hour	Summary of Events and Information	Remarks and references to Appendices
Middle Camp. W.	1917 June 1st		32nd Bttn The Royal Fusiliers. Weather clear Bright & Warm. The Battalion supplied men for day & night working Parties	N.1 & 0.8.
"	2nd		Weather Clean & fine. Normal working parties found. One Stone found. Working Party of 31st / 1st June. O.C. Coy reconnoitred route to assembly trenches. Officers entered by the Battalion 1/c Party, "having behaved and worked splendidly" under enemy fire in front line.	
"	3rd		Weather clear Bright & warm. Open air Divine Service during morning. Normal working Parties supplied.	
"	4th		Weather clear & fine. Battn to RENINGHELST allotted as to the Battalion. G.O.C. in the coming operations. In the afternoon the C/O conferred with all Officers taking part in the attack and went over the scheme of operations with them. Open air Concert by Battalion Concert Party.	
"	5th		Battalion moved the lines leaving Camp at 6 am & the other two Coys at 10 p.m. A. Coy took up Battle front in front line 0.2.8 – 0.3.2 & support. D " " the R line. H.Q. Convent Lane. B. & C Coys Advanced G.H.Q. 2nd line. Details of the Battalion formed the Reinforcement Camp at RENINGHELST. Weather clear bright & warm.	

WAR DIARY
or
INTELLIGENCE SUMMARY

(Erase heading not required.)

Army Form C. 2118.

Sheet I

32nd Bttn Royal Fusiliers

Place	Date	Hour	Summary of Events and Information	Remarks and references to Appendices
In the Line	6th	10pm	The Battalion remained in its position during the day and at 10pm commenced to occupy their assembly positions for the attack. (Weather clear & fine.)	J.H.
"	7th		Battalion assumed position of assembly two hours prior to the attack. Report on action attached. Weather clear & fine.	J.H.
Elzenwalle Camp	8th		Battalion were relieved at 2 am by the "Buffs" 24th Div and marched to G.H.Q. 2nd Line. Day spent in cleaning up and resting. Battalion moved to Elzenwalle Camp in the Evening.	J.H.
"	9th		Details rejoined Battalion at Elzenwalle Camp during the morning. Battalion Roll called. Weather Clear, Bright & Warm.	J.H.
"	10th		Open air Divine Service. Burying & Salvaging Parties found by Battalion. Coy Officers reconnoitred new Line.	J.H.
"	11th		Battalion relieved the 7th Northamptons of the 73rd Brigade, 23rd Middlesex Regt and part of the 20th D.L.I. of the 123rd Bde. 13th Bde B & C Coys Reserve Line (Black Line) between S.W. corner of Denys Wood and Trench Junction at O.10.c.35.95. D.Coy (Blue Line) between O.9.c.25. & O.9.c.3.1. A.Coy Old German Line between Oasis Street O.9.a.40.95. and Oesthoek Estaminet. Batt H.Q. Dammstrasse O.9.c.25.80.	O.9.c.25.80 J.H.

WAR DIARY
or
INTELLIGENCE SUMMARY

(Erase heading not required.)

Army Form C. 2118.

Sheet 3.

Place	Date	Hour	Summary of Events and Information	Remarks and references to Appendices
In Support to Right Bde Sector	12th		32nd Bn Royal Fusiliers Enemy Artillery very active on the whole of the Brigade area. Enemy Aircraft active. Flying low over our front line trenches and firing at garrison. Explosion was heard near the ruins at O.II.a.0.2. Cleaning up & salvaging carried out.	O.O.C 25.80. HR
	13th		Enemy Artillery very active. In the evening in retaliation for two of our practice barrages shoots he shelled RAVINE WOOD heavily. Our patrols went out advancing 600 yards without encountering the enemy. Our heavy guns caused an explosion in the enemy's lines. Enemy aircraft active	HR
	14th		Enemy Artillery Active, special attention being paid to DENYS WOOD, THE RAVINE & THE BLUE LINE. Enemy Aircraft active.	HR
	15th		Enemy Artillery Active, especially on left subsector area. Enemy Aircraft active.	HR
R C Sub Sector	16		Enemy Artillery very active, 9.40 p.m. the Germans put up a heavy barrage on OLIVE TRENCH and bombarded the DELBSKE FARM locality vigorously. Our Artillery promptly replied. Battalion moved to the Front Line in Relief of the 10th Bn Queen's R W Surrey Regt. Heavy enemy shelling caused difficulty relief but obstacles suffered	HR

Army Form C. 2118.

WAR DIARY
or
INTELLIGENCE SUMMARY

(Erase heading not required.)

SHEET 4.

Place	Date	Hour	Summary of Events and Information	Remarks and references to Appendices
Rt 2nd Sector	17/4		32nd Bn The Royal Fusiliers Enemy Artillery active. Attention being paid to DENYS WOOD. Enemy Aircraft active early in the morning. Our Patrols went out. No sounds of the enemy were heard.	C.H.H.
"	18th		Enemy Artillery very active chiefly on RAVINE & DENYS WOOD. Enemy aircraft active. Our Patrols went out to reconnoitre valley in front of our line no enemy were encountered.	C.H.H.
"	19th		Enemy artillery less active. Two large fires were seen behind the enemy lines. Enemy transport lines on VIERSTRAAT ROAD were shelled, causing casualties. Transport lines moved to M.G. 6.1.7. near RENINGHELST. Inter Coy relief carried out to-day.	C.H.H.
"	20th		Enemy Artillery comparatively quiet. Enemy aircraft very active. Much smoke was seen rising from KORTEWILDE, TEN BRIELEN and the villages during the morning. North of the ROOZEBEEK was twice patrolled. No movements of the enemy were heard.	C.H.H.
"	21st		Enemy Artillery active. Enemy Aircraft active. Our patrols went out to examine edges of GREEN WOOD, no sounds of enemy were heard.	C.H.H.

WAR DIARY
INTELLIGENCE SUMMARY

Army Form C. 2118.

Sheet 5.

Place	Date	Hour	Summary of Events and Information	Remarks and references to Appendices
	22nd		32nd Bttn. The Royal Fusiliers. Enemy Artillery very active. The enemy appeared to have more guns in action. A large fire was seen in the direction of WARNETON. Battalion relieved by the 21st K.R.R. Corps & moved back to Support position in the Blue Line & the DAMMSTRASSE. Relief being completed by Midnight.	I.SS
IN SUPPORT	23rd		Enemy artillery active. Our artillery very active. Enemy aircraft less active. Working Parties found for improving the Black line. This continued to dawn in villages behind the enemy lines.	I.SS
"	24th		Enemy artillery less active. Aircraft active. Working Parties found for consolidating Communication Trenches.	I.SS
"	25th		Enemy artillery active. Working Parties found. Our aircraft active. Several fires seen burning behind the enemy's lines.	I.SS
"	26		Enemy Artillery very active. Our artillery active. Battalion relieved the 10th Queens in the line. Left Sub Sector. Relief being completed at 2 a.m. During the relief the Battn. H.Q. shelled with daybreak. Enemy put over a large number of shells causing casualties.	I.SS
Left Sub Sector	27th		Enemy Artillery active. Enemy Aircraft active. Our patrols went out to ascertain the nature about of the enemy. None of the enemy were seen. Our Lewis guns were fired at a considerable distance behind his line. his front line being about 75 Coast of Stony Fine on Shell holes. The movement of the enemy appeared to indicate that he was at work consolidating his line of defence along the East Bank of the YPRES-COMINES CANAL	I.SS

Army Form C. 2118.

WAR DIARY
or
INTELLIGENCE SUMMARY

Sheet 6.

(Erase heading not required.)

Instructions regarding War Diaries and Intelligence Summaries are contained in F. S. Regs., Part II and the Staff Manual respectively. Title Pages will be prepared in manuscript.

Place	Date	Hour	Summary of Events and Information	Remarks and references to Appendices
Left Side Sector	28th		32nd Bttn Royal Fusiliers. Enemy artillery very active. Our patrols went out reconnoitre to Mans Land. None of the enemy were seen this side of GREEN WOOD. A severe thunderstorm broke out during the evening accompanied by a heavy downpour of rain.	AH
"	29th		Enemy Artillery active. Battalion relieved by the 21st London Regt in the Left Sub Sectn. relief of evening completed at 2.50 am	AH
	30th		Battalion marched to Camp at M.L.d.S.B. halting on the way for breakfast at Ridgewood and arriving at Camp at 6.30 am. Weather very wet. Morning spent in resting and cleaning up. Battalion moved off to the METEREN AREA in the evening leaving Camp at 8 pm and arriving at METEREN at 1am the following morning and proceeded to fill up billets in the Town	AH

CASUALTIES during June 1917

	OFFICERS	O. RANKS
Killed	2	19
Wounded	4	151
Died of Wounds	-	5
Missing	-	2

CASUALTIES during the action June 7th 1917.

	Officers	O. Ranks
Killed	2	24
Wounded	7	183
Missing	1	2
Died of Wounds	-	8

Strength Summary

	Off	O. Ranks
Maximum	35	955
Minimum	26	728
Present	21	737

AH
Capt Adjt.
32nd Royal Fusiliers

REPORT ON OPERATIONS.

June 7th, 1917.

32nd (S) Bn The ROYAL FUSILIERS.

1. ARMY SCHEME.

The 2nd Army assumed the offensive on the 7th June, 1917, from S.E. of YPRES to PLOEGSTEERT WOOD. The 41st Divisional Front from right to left was:-
(1st Stage)   124th Infy Bde, 123rd Infy Bde.
(2nd Stage)   124th Infy Bde, 122nd Infy Bde.
The three objectives, which were respectively the "RED LINE", "BLUE LINE" and "BLACK LINE", are shewn on the attached map.

2. BRIGADE SCHEME.

The Brigade was disposed for the attack as follows:-
On the right.....10th Bn "Queens" R.W.S. Regt.
In the centre....21st K.R.R. Corps.
On the left......32nd Bn Royal Fusiliers - from Trench O.2.7. central to O.3.2. central.
"   "   .....26th Bn Royal Fusiliers, within the same limits.

3. BATTALION OBJECTIVES.

1st Objective - The enemy's front and support lines, including Nos. 4 & 5 Craters, from OASIS DRIVE (inclusive) on the right to OASIS STREET (exclusive) on the left (RED LINE).

Final Objective - After passing through the 26th Royal Fusiliers at the DAMMSTRASSE (which was their objective) the three trenches, OBSTACLE AVENUE, OBSTACLE SUPPORT and OBSTACLE SWITCH, from GOUDEZENE FARM (exclusive) on the right to a point on OBSTACLE SWITCH 250 yds to the left (BLACK LINE).

4. ASSEMBLY.

Immediately prior to the action the Battalion was disposed in depth, from the front line trenches as far back as G.H.Q. Advanced Line. The movement to the assembly position was commenced at 5 hours before ZERO.
The assembly of the Battalion took longer and was more difficult than was anticipated owing to congestion in the trenches and enemy shell fire. One Sergeant and 2 Other Ranks were wounded on the way, and several casualties occurred actually in the position. However the Battalion was up to time and all stores distributed for carrying over.

5. DISPOSITION.

Opposite ST. ELOI CRATERS, North of MESSINES RIDGE, from Trench O.2.6 (opposite No. 4 Crater) inclusive to Trench O.3.2, 500 yards left, in 4 waves, 2 waves being in the Front Trench and 2 waves behind the parados. On our right a gap to allow for the explosion of mines under Nos. 2 & 3 Craters, with the 21st K.R.R. Corps beyond. On our left the 23rd Middlesex Regt, being the Right Battalion of the 123rd Brigade.

6. ADVANCE.

General direction 157° true bearing. The 4 waves were at only 20 yards distance to enable the 26th Royal Fusiliers, immediately in rear, to clear our Front Line before the enemy's barrage dropped on it.

7. NARRATIVE.

There was a bright enough moon to cause anxiety about the discovery by the enemy of our move. Very lights were being sent up frequently from the enemy craters and Support Line. About 15 minutes before Zero rockets bursting into a shower a orange coloured stars were sent up from the Crater almost continually, one after another. These lights were also being sent up by the enemy well away to our left.

At 10 minutes before Zero Headquarters moved into NO MAN'S-LAND with the left two thirds of each of the 4 waves, the right remaining in the assembly position to avoid the shock of the mines to be exploded under the ST ELOI Craters 200 yards to the right front of the Battalion. The enemy signals were still going up and at ZERO hour the mines were successfully exploded and the Battalion went forward to our barrage rapidly, the enemy's barrage opening simultaneously on our Front Line and part of NO MAN'S LAND. One officer (2nd Lieut. HARRISON) was wounded at this time.

The Battalion went without check to the RED LINE, meeting with practically no opposition. The direction was good, though the left was overlapped slightly by the 23rd Middlesex. Casualties were very slight.
The whole ground and enemy trenches in this neighbourhood were so ruined by our shell fire as to be practically unrecognisable, and a part of the Battalion, in the excessive keenness which they showed throughout, went on with the 26th Bn Royal Fusiliers right up to the DAMMSTRASSE and took part in the assault of it. The Stream marking the right of the RED LINE had been converted by our shell fire into merely a string of shell craters having more water in them than those in the neighbourhood.

The Battalion was reorganised here and dug in, with the Vickers Guns and Stokes Mortars , and Headquarters were established for the time being in a shell hole immediately behind its left.

At 5.40 am the Battalion moved up to the PURPLE LINE and collected those who had gone forward. At 6.50 am the advance from the DAMMSTRASSE was begun under the barrage for the attack on the BLACK LINE, which was reached under cover of the barrage at schedule time, viz. 8.10 am.
The three trenches - OBSTACLE AVENUE, OBSTACLE SUPPORT and OBSTACLE SWITCH - which were taken in this final advance, had been battered almost out of recognition by our shell fire, and practically no opposition was offered. A number of the enemy fled and were fired upon, most of them being accounted for either by our rifle fire or shell fire. Only about 30 were left to be taken prisoners - these mostly were eager to give themselves up, but a few required bombing out of their dugouts. One German Officer was seen to shoot himself in a dugout.

During the ½ hour halt between OBSTACLE AVENUE and OBSTACLE SUPPORT a defensive flank was formed on the right facing the ESTAMINET and firing into the enemy retreating therefrom, until the K.R.R. Corps took the position. The flank formation then swung into line again and joined in the attack on the last two trenches.

The Battalion dug itself in about 100 yards beyond OBSTACLE SWITCH between its correct boundaries and sent out a line of advanced posts with 7 Lewis Guns. Patrols were pushed out and small parties of the enemy observed in ROSE WOOD and the neighbourhood of ODYSSEY TRENCH were kept under our rifle and machine gun fire and many casualties caused. A few guns were seen being taken away in the distance and were also fired on. Two Vickers Guns reached the BLACK LINE with the Battalion and took up a position one on each flank. A party of R.E. arrived later on and constructed a strong point in our

NARRATIVE (Contd)

Front Line.

We got into touch with the 21st K.R.R. Corps on the right and the 12th East Surreys on the left immediately on arrival on the BLACK LINE. *About 4pm Bn H.Q. were established in CESTRELE SWITCH immediately in rear of GOUDEZHUNE FARM*

8. OUR ARTILLERY.

The barrages throughout were entirely satisfactory and the few casualties caused by them were only due to the mens eagerness to push forward. There is no doubt that the power and precision of our artillery during both the preliminary bombardment and the action itself enabled the infantry to carry out the programme without the slightest hitch. The accurate shooting not only destroyed the enemy's defences and morale of his men, but inspired our troops with the confidence which is necessary for complete success.

9. ENEMY ARTILLERY.

During the assembly his enfilade fire from the North East caused one or two casualties. At Zero minus 2 minutes his barrage began to open on our front trench and part of NO MAN'S LAND, in response to the rocket calls sent up from his Craters during the preceding 15 minutes, causing several casualties, including one officer - 2nd Lt. GOSLING (killed). During the action the Battalion was well beyond his barrage, which seemed poor and ineffective. He devoted a good deal of attention to our original trenches and communications, with a view to cutting off reinforcements. After the capture of the DAMMSTRASSE his shelling of that line and the RED LINE, where the Battalion spent two hours, was weak and the two hours wait caused us no serious trouble. After the capture of the BLACK LINE our troops holding it were not inconvenienced by his shell fire at all, though he searched the ground between them and the DAMMSTRASSE with Whizz-bangs and kept OASIS DRIVE under the fire of his 4.2s. He was obviously searching for our advanced 18 pounder positions with heavier shells, but having lost observation made poor shooting.

10. COMMUNICATIONS.

The Battalion signallers, under 2nd Lieut. HOME-GALL, with the invaluable help of Sergt SCOBLE, did most excellent work throughout. On arrival at the RED LINE Battalion Headquarters were established in a shell hole 50 yards behind the left of it, and the power buzzer was immediately brought into position and messages sent to Brigade Forward Command Post. A line was laid to the Brigade Forward Station 30 minutes after Zero and communication was in good working order by telephone at that time, also be Lucas lamp to Divisional Visual Station at H.36d. 8.2.

A wire was started towards the 123rs Brigade Forward Station at RUINED FARM, but owing to dust and smoke direction was lost. A linesman however connected up with "B" Detachment 123rd Brigade. Visual signalling was carried on between Battalion Headquarters and the Companies at the other end of the RED LINE. At Zero plus 30 minutes Battn Headquarters moved up to a point 50 yards behind the left of the DAMMSTRASSE, the power buzzer being handed over th "B" Detachment Brigade Forward Station. Communication was established by telephone with that Detachment within a few minutes. Several messages were sent to aeroplanes by panel, and all Companies were in touch by visual. A disc message asking for lengthening of barrage of the BLUE LINE opposite PHEASANT WOOD was picked up and transmitted by

COMMUNICATIONS (Contd)

telephone to C.E. (183rd Brigade), and by aeroplane panel to contact plane. The message reached the Brigade and was promptly acted upon. Several messages from the Battalion on the left were transmitted through our station to the 123rd Brigade Headquarters. On the advance from the DAMMSTRASSE the Battalion Signalling Sergeant and the 2 linesmen followed the last wave, laying out wire, and 5 minutes after the capture of the Black Line were in direct communication with Battalion Headquarters. Shortly afterwards the Battalion Headquarters moved up to DAMMWOOD and a line from there was linked on to this line, thus establishing communication with all Companies and with Brigade Forward Party.

Note. On arrival at the RED LINE the man in charge of the aeroplane panel was temporarily missing, but successful communication with aeroplane was established by waving signalling flags parallel to the ground.

11. MEDICAL ARRANGEMENTS.

4 Stretcher bearers per Company advanced with the Battalion, 12 extra stretcher bearers remained with the Battalion M.O. at the R.A.P. These latter were pushed forward by him some 1½ hours after zero and cleared the ground forward. The scheme worked out satisfactorily, all wounded were got away in reasonable time and the R.A.P. was never over-crowded.

12. AIRCRAFT.

One or two enemy machines were seen overhead and a pair of them brought down one of our machines, but there were large numbers of our machines in action and no enemy machine was able to fly low over our troops. The contact planes were continually in evidence and we got several messages taken by them besides the flare signals.

13. TANKS.

Only one tank reached the Battalion final objective, the remainder on the Brigade Front all broke down either before reaching the DAMMSTRASSE or just after. The going was obviously almost impossible for them, and it is astonishing that some of them got as far as they did. Their services were fortunately never required.

14. CASUALTIES.

The casualties were slight and practically all occurred before leaving the DAMMSTRASSE. Of the 6 officer casualties four occurred near the enemy front line. The total casualties are 6 officers and 163 other ranks, including 29 at present unaccounted for. (None fell into the enemy's hands) The strength going into action was 17 officers and 551 other ranks.

Lt. Col. commdg
32nd (S) Bn The Royal Fusiliers.

10.6.17.

WAR DIARY or INTELLIGENCE SUMMARY

Army Form C. 2118.

32=(S) Battn THE ROYAL FUSILIERS

Sheet T.

Place	Date	Hour	Summary of Events and Information	Remarks and references to Appendices
METEREN	1917 July 1st		The Battalion arrived at METEREN at 1 a.m this morning having marched from the RENINGHELST AREA, the journey taking 5 hours. The Billets were in the village of METEREN itself. after a rest, cleaning up occupied the remainder of the day.	X.15.D.37 Map Sheet 27 S.E.
"	2nd		Ironing under Company arrangements was carried out during the morning, the rest of the day being free for rest & recreation. In the evening the Divisional Concert Party "The CRUMPS" gave a performance for the Battn in the Y.M.C.A. The day was bright & warm.	"
"	3rd		The morning was devoted to Specialist training + Coy organisation. Football in the aft. Six Officers were posted to the Battn + arrived from the 39th Inf Base Depot today. The weather remained clear + warm. A draft of 120 O.R. (trained Specialists) arrived today.	"
"	4th		The usual Specialist training + Coy organisation under Company arrangements were carried out. Instruction in bayonet fighting was given by Colonel CHEETHAM of the 17th Army Gymnastic Staff on the Battalion Parade Ground.	"
"	5th		The Range at NOOTE BOOM was allotted for Musketry practice during the morning and this was carried out under Company arrangements. Specialist training in the afternoon.	"

WAR DIARY
or
INTELLIGENCE SUMMARY

Army Form C. 2118.

32nd (S.) Batt. Royal Fusiliers.

Sheet 11

(Erase heading not required.)

Place	Date	Hour	Summary of Events and Information	Remarks and references to Appendices
METEREN	1917 July 6th		Weather continues good. Instruction in Lewis gun was given to Officers by the Lewis gun Officer – Bayonet fighting practice was carried out under the The Army Gymnastic Instructor. The following M.C.'s had been announced in Corps Routine Orders of this date as being awarded honors for gallantry & devotion to duty during the action on 7th gravity at ST ELOI:— Bar to Military Medal 22347 Sgt W.T. SCOBLE, 22353 Pte T. CASS, 24614 L/Cpl E.L. BARTLETT. Military Medal. 22102 Sgt. C.H. CAMERON, 53016 Sgt. F.N. JOHNSON, (since died of Wounds) 22531 Sgt. F.D. MURCHIE. 21176 L/Sgt. S.A. CLARK, 49729 Cpl I.A. DRAPKIN, 60079 Cpl R.J. PETERS, 60237 Cpl W.C.H. PRICE, 8247 L/Cpl A.E.H. YATES, 34738 Pte C.W. PRICE, 11109 Pte F.G. WESTON, 44604 Pte A. CLARK.	X.15 D.37. (Sheet 27.S.E)
"	7th		Battalion Parade in the morning on Battn. Parade Ground. Training under Coy arrangements was carried out. The Commanding Officer Lt. Col W.C. CLARK, was awarded D.S.O. for gallantry in action & splendid leadership during the Battle of St Boi on 7th June 1917.	"
"	8th		Divine Service was held on the Battalion Parade Ground followed by a celebration of Holy Communion. Decorations were announced in C.R.O. of today, as follows:— Military Cross. 2nd Lt. ARTHUR KELLER DAVIS and 2nd Lt EDWARD REGINALD HOME-GALL, D.C.M. C.S.M. J.T. JACKSON.	"

2449 Wt. W14957/M90 750,000 1/16 J.B.C. & A. Forms/C.2118/12.

WAR DIARY
INTELLIGENCE SUMMARY

32nd (S.) Batt. Royal Fusiliers.

Sheet III

Army Form C. 2118.

Place	Date	Hour	Summary of Events and Information	Remarks and references to Appendices
METEREN	July 9th		Weather continues bright & sunshiny. Specialist training & Coy organisation were carried out under the usual arrangements.	X.15.D.37 (Map Sheet 27 Œ)
"	10th		Training & minor Company arrangements were continued. A letter from the Divisional Commander was received conveying his appreciation of the good work and cheerful and soldierly spirit shewn by all ranks under the severe strain and during retaliatory fire while holding the line for three weeks past.	"
"	11th		Battalion Parade on Battalion Parade ground. 2 Companies (A + B) were ordered to proceed to RIDGEWOOD today in relief of 11th Bn R.W.Kents for work under X Corps Signals. Weather continued fine.	"
"	12th		The morning was spent in preparation & rehearsal for presentation of awards by the Divisional Commander in the afternoon. Battalion paraded at 2 p.m. on Battalion Parade ground & he presented to the recipients the ribbons of their awards. Afterwards the Divl Commander inspected the 1st Line Transport which he expressed his satisfaction at the cleanliness of the vehicles & condition of its animals. A letter was received subsequently conveying the G.O.C appreciation of the smart appearance of the Batt.c at the Parade.	"

2449 Wt. W14957/M90 750,000 1/16 J.B.C. & A. Forms/C.2118/12.

WAR DIARY
or
INTELLIGENCE SUMMARY
(Erase heading not required.)

Army Form C. 2118.

32nd (S.) Batt. Royal Fusiliers

Sheet IV

Place	Date	Hour	Summary of Events and Information	Remarks and references to Appendices
METEREN and	July 13th		The remainder of the Battalion moved by march route to RIDGEWOOD, leaving METEREN at 10 a.m. and arriving at RIDGEWOOD at 4 p.m. The Battalion were accommodated in the former dug out occupied during the late mouth. Spent the night huts and Bivouacs. On reaching RIDGEWOOD a draft of 68 o.r. joined the	x.159.3.7 Map Sheet 27.S.E.
RIDGEWOOD			Battalion having been posted from the 63rd (R.N.) Div. Base Depot. The weather was hot & close throughout the day. GHQ	N.5.A.5.2 (Map Sheet 28.S.W.)
RIDGEWOOD	14th		The Battalion provided working parties for Cable burying & trench digging in the vicinity of SPOIL BANK and THE BLUFF under En. Coy. R.E. Signals. GHQ	N.5.A.5.2 (Map Sheet 28.S.W.)
	15th		The usual working parties were provided. During the night 15/16th we had two casualties, consisting of 1 Officer & two caught by Enemy shell fire & suffers 17 casualties. 16 other ranks, two of the latter subsequently dying of their wounds. Enemy aircraft was quite active during the day & in the Early morning flew quite low over the Camp. Our Lewis guns gave them attention. GHQ	"
	16th		Working parties were supplied for work on Cable burying. During the night Enemy aircraft were over the Camp & bombs were dropped at a distance. In some unknown village. The enemy made repeated efforts to bring down by a new kind of Shrapnel one of our observation Balloon at HAZEBROUCK, but failed to do so. The Observer dropped by parachute on an enemy plane approach.	

WAR DIARY
or
INTELLIGENCE SUMMARY
32nd (S.) Batt. Royal Fusiliers.

Sheet V

Army Form C. 2118.

(Erase heading not required.)

Place	Date	Hour	Summary of Events and Information	Remarks and references to Appendices
RIDGEWOOD	1917 July 17th		Day & night working parties were supplied by the Battalion. A draft of 124 other ranks was received from the Base (21 or from the 1/22nd London Regt & 103 or from the 3rd Batn Kings Liverpool Regt.) Work was continued on the allotments at RIDGEWOOD by 3 men of the Battn.	N.5.A. 6.2 (Maps Sheet 28.SW.)
"	18th		The usual working parties were supplied for the 7th Corps Report. Two Companies of the 10th Bn Queen's arrived during the afternoon to assist in supply by working parties & came under the command of the Battalion. Enemy aircraft were active. The weather became unsettled with gales at intervals throughout the day.	"
"	19th		Working parties as usual from the Battalion and from the 2 Coys of the Queen's. Specialist Training was carried out by the rest of the Battn who were not engaged in working parties. Hostile aircraft were again active. Our bombardment continues.	"
"	20th		Usual working parties were supplied, the remainder of the Battn carrying out Company of aviation.	"
"	21st		Working parties were supplied. In the afternoon a Battalion Parade was held at which the C.O. distributed the cards of appreciation from the Div'l Commander.	"

WAR DIARY
INTELLIGENCE SUMMARY

32nd (S.) Batt. Royal Fusiliers.

Sheet VI.

Army Form C. 2118.

Place	Date	Hour	Summary of Events and Information	Remarks and references to Appendices
RIDGEWOOD	1917 July 22nd		Usual working parties were supplied. Specialist training was continued. A draft of 60 other ranks arrived from the 3rd 4th Inf. Depot having been transferred from the West Riding Regt. A letter was received from the G.O.C. expressing his satisfaction of the pleasant manner in which the Officers & men of the Batt'n Carried out their work in the after noon of the 15/16th instant. The G.O.C. signified his appreciation of the excellent discipline shown.	N.5.A.5.2 (Map Sheet 28.S.W.)
"	23rd		Working parties were again supplied. Supplies for Cattle carrying under 3rd Corps R.E. Signals. Enemy aircraft was active throughout the day. Our Bombardment was continued to 4th coming operations continued. Some gas shells fell near the Camp during the night but they were ineffective. The day was clear & fine.	"
"	24th		Usual working parties were supplied. The C/O proceeded to take over Command of the 1st 4th Inf Bde, & Major H.A. ROBINSON, D.S.O. assumed Command of the Battalion. RIDGEWOOD was slightly shelled by the enemy during the night with H.E. & Shrapnel. Enemy planes dropping bombs in the direction of BAILLEUL during the night.	"
RIDGEWOOD AND DE ZON CAMP LA CLYTTE	25th		The Battalion proceeded by march route to DE ZON CAMP arriving there at 5 p.m. The day was wet & stormy throughout.	M.12.c.6.3 (Map Sheet 28.S.W.)

Army Form C. 2118.

WAR DIARY
or
INTELLIGENCE SUMMARY

32nd (S.) Batt. Royal Fusiliers.

Sheet VII.

(Erase heading not required.)

Place	Date	Hour	Summary of Events and Information	Remarks and references to Appendices
DE ZON CAMP LA CLYTTE	1917 July 26th		The day was spent in cleaning up & training with Company arrangements, lectures being given in explanation of the forth coming operations. Enemy aircraft were again active during the evening dropping bombs in the region of BAILLEUL. JFS	M.12.c.6.8 (Map Sheet 28 S.W.)
"	27th		Company Organisation & Specialist training was carried on during the morning. Lectures in the afternoon. JFS	"
"	28th		In the afternoon a practice attack was carried out by each Company. The final of the Bdn football Sta Cup Platoon Competition has to be postponed. JFS	1
"	29th		Weather Continues Showery. The Rifle Sermont Range near WEST OUTRE has also to be closed for practising the firing of rifle grenades. The Open air Church Parade has to be abandoned owing to the heavy downpours of rain. A concert was given in the evening to the Battn. Band. The DIEHARDS which amused them considerably. JFS	

2449 Wt. W14957/M90 750,000 1/16 J.B.C. & A. Forms/C.2118/12.

Army Form C. 2118.

WAR DIARY
or
INTELLIGENCE SUMMARY

(Erase heading not required.)

32nd (S.) Batt. Royal Fusiliers.

Sheet VIII.

Place	Date	Hour	Summary of Events and Information	Remarks and references to Appendices
DE ZON CAMP.	1917 July 30th		Weather cloudy. Overcast with light rain at intervals. The Baths at MURRUMBIDGEE CAMP were allotted to the Batt. today. The Batt. proceeded to the VOORMEZEELE AREA leaving Camp at 9 p.m. & arrived at their destination at 10.10 p.m. Details were left at DE ZON CAMP with Capt. R.W. HAMMOND in command.	M.12.c.6.3. (Map Sheet 28 S.W.)
VOORMEZEELE	31st	3.30	Weather very hot & close. The Battalion were in Reserve for the Attack today occupying the following positions:— (a) MIDDLESEX LANE from G.H.Q. 2nd Line to VOORMEZEELE SWITCH (b) G.H.Q. 2nd Line from BRASSERIE – ELZENWALLE ROAD to MIDDLESEX LANE. Battalion Headquarters were established in G.H.Q. 2nd Line at H.8.C.7.4. Casualties during the day were 2 killed 1 died of wounds 36 wounds all O.R.	

STRENGTH during the Month.

		Offrs	O.R.
MAXIMUM strength during month		38	971
MINIMUM " " "		31	757
PRESENT " " "		38	964

CASUALTIES during the month of July.

	Offrs	O.R.
Killed	—	2
Wounded	1	29
Missing	—	—
Died of Wounds	—	3

[Signature]
Capt & Adjt.
32nd (S.) Batt. Royal Fusiliers.

32nd. (S) Battn. THE ROYAL FUSILIERS.

REPORT ON ENEMY ATTACK ON MORNING 5th AUGUST 1917, ON BATTALION FRONT.

PRELIMINARY BOMBARDMENT. 1. At 2 am the enemy commenced shelling our forward area heavily. At 3.3 am this increased to an intense bombardment, with shelling of back areas.

WEATHER. 2. At this period and throughout the action, there was dense fog.

LISTENING POST. 3. At 4 am the advanced Listening post in front of our left Company withdrew to our front line with information that the enemy was advancing on our line.

ENEMY ATTACK. 4. Ten minutes later the barrage lifted on our Support line and the attack developed under cover of the fog and smoke bombs. So far as this Battalion is concerned, the attack was confined to the left half, the extent to the left of that not being known. The frontal attack was held off by rifle and Lewis Gun fire, but a break through on the right of the Battalion on our left allowed a party to get behind our line. Half a dozen of the enemy were dealt with there and several further attempts were made on our front and left flank, but the line was held in its entirety and the attack stopped at 6 am.

REINFORCEMENTS. 5. Major Robinson who had been inspecting the line during the night and was present throughout the action, went back and brought back personally two platoons from the supports during the attack. Other reinforcements were sent up from Battn. H.Q. (vice para. 8.)

ENEMY DIGGING IN. 6. After 6 am. the enemy were seen to be digging themselves in on a line about 150 yards in front of the left half Battalion and he opened machine gun fire which rendered movement difficult and caused casualties. This was replied to by rifle and Lewis gun fire which was seen to cause him losses, as was the case with our rifle fire during the attack itself, the men having made such use of them that they became too hot to hold and several bolts jammed. The enemy's digging was interfered with as much as possible.

SITUATION NORMAL. 7. By 6.30 am the situation had become normal, though it was uncertain what the position on the left flank was. It was ascertained at midday that the enemy occupied about 100 yards of JEHOVAH TRENCH, viz. north of the Klein-Zillebeke road.

COMMUNICATION 8. At 4 am the enemy's barrage was suspected of being on our front, but the only means of communication besides runners, viz. visual, was rendered impossible by the fog. A power buzzer sent up the day before had not yet been got into working order. The first information from the front line was received by runner at 5.35 am.

(1)

REINFORCEMENTS FROM H.Q.	9.	Two platoons were forthwith ordered up from the reserve Coy. under Capt. Thorburn, who was instructed to carry out a counter attack if neccessary, otherwise to remain as a reinforcement. The two supporting platoons of the Left Coy. were found to have been called up by the Battalion on our left and were not available. This situation arose from the fact that the position taken over by them from the outgoing Battalion was west of the Klein Zillebeke Road, therefore out of our area. At 5.50 am a telephone line was run out from Bn. H.Q. to the visual station at I.36.d.05.65 and half an hour later the Battn. Signalling Officer was sent out to lay on a new line from there to the front line. By 7 am communication was through but very shortly the wire to the Visual station from H.Q's was cut to piecess. Both Battn. & Coy. runners were used freely after 6 am and rendered valuable service though slow.
ARTILLERY. (ENEMY)	10.	The bombardment was very severe and the whole area back to Bn. H.Q's was heavily shelled rendering the movement of reinforcements difficult
OUR ARTILLERY	11.	At 4.30 am a slow rate of fire was obtained through the Artillery Laision Officer and shortly after county battery work was begun. The enemy however did not decrease his fire and counter battery work was continued until midday.

MENTION.	12.	I wish to draw your attention to the fine behaviour of the Officers and men concerned in repelling the counter attack. Major Robinson D.S O who was inspecting the line at the time, organised the defence and took a personal share in the fighting, particularly when leading a few men against the party of the enemy which had got round to the rear of the centre post in the forward line and killing half of them and dispersing the remainder, after both the Lewis Guns on his flanks had been put out of action. His already proved qualities as a fighting soldier made his presence invaluable and his courage and coolness were most inspiring. I cannot speak too highly of this Officer.
		Capt. H.L. KIRBY. commanding the Company involved shewed most splendid courage and resource. He was severely wounded by a bullet in the hand early in the action, but carried on until well after the situation had become normal, in spite of severe pain.
		2nd Lieut G.W. MURRELL was severely wounded in three places in the right hand and arm, but carried on through the action and was eventually the only officer on that sector not being relieved until 12 hours after the attack. His behaviour and personal bravery was splendid throughout.
		The other officers concerned, who also did very fine work were:-
		    2nd Lieut G.F. COOK (Killed)
		    " " H.W. HUTTON who was wounded but carried on.
		    " " F.H. KENNER (Wounded in the shoulder and carried on)
		    A/Capt. J.M. THORBURN who brought up reinforcements from the

MENTION (Contd)
Reserve Company and was very severely wounded, (Since died of wounds)

OFFICER CASUALTIES.
Killed..............1.
Died of Wounds......1.
Wounded............4.

REPORT by Sergt. CLARK.

About a quarter to four our advanced bombing post sent back warning by a runner that enemy were advancing on left front. The Post fired and withdrew to the Strong Post Line, when the Lewis Guns and rifles opened fire. Major ROBINSON sent me about 4 am on right flank with Lewis Gun team. I had not until then seen any of the enemy. About 4.10 am a barrage was dropped all round the Strong Point and kept on for 10 minutes, when it lifted to Support Line. I then heard our men open fire, which was maintained for several minutes. I could still see no signs of the enemy and posted one team thus:-

Myself and No. 1 watching front.
2 men half right. 1 man half left, and 1 man watching rear. The first warning I had that they were behind us was from the man watching behind, who shouted and fell forward. I saw about 12 Germans advancing towards us from the rear, having got round our left flank. We fired a magazine at them with the Lewis Gun and withdrew towards the Support Line, as we were not in touch with anything. We withdrew about 10 yards at a time and opened fire at each halt. When we reaching Support Line they were "standing to" but had not seen the "S.O.S". I told Sgt FOSTER and he gave me a runner to go to B.H.Q. The Lewis Gun team were attached to Support Line.

WAR DIARY
or
INTELLIGENCE SUMMARY
(Erase heading not required.)

Army Form C. 2118.

32 R F (SERVICE) BATTⁿ FUS Vol 16 Sheet I

Place	Date	Hour	Summary of Events and Information	Remarks and references to Appendices
	1917 August 1st		Battalion in Divisional Reserve for attack. Weather- Very wet & cold	H.36.c.9.4
"	2nd		Battalion remained in position. Enemy artillery active. Weather continued to be unsettled.	C.3.1
"	3rd		Weather slightly improved. Battalion marched to position during morning. In the afternoon & evening Companies moved up to relieve 26th R. Fusiliers (124th) & 21st K.R.R. Corps in the Front line. Enemy artillery very active, causing casualties.	C.01
KLEIN ZILLEBEKE	4th		Relief completed. Battalion holding line in the neighbourhood of KLEIN ZILLEBEKE. The B.O.C. received a communication from the Army Commander saying he was fully conscious of the stiff time the officers & men were having & that he was being pleased with the spirit shewn by all ranks."	C.01
"	5th		At dawn enemy made strong counter-attack under cover of thick mist. Report on attack attached. Enemy artillery very active throughout the day, causing many casualties. Weather fine	C.01
"	6th		On the night 6/7th Battⁿ was relieved by the 2nd K.R.R. Corps. Enemy artillery active, gas shells being shot over during relief.	C.01

WAR DIARY
INTELLIGENCE SUMMARY

Sheet II

Army Form C. 2118.

Place	Date	Hour	Summary of Events and Information	Remarks and references to Appendices
	1917 August 7th		Relief completed at 5 a.m. Battn in rest camp in neighbourhood of ELZENWALLE CHATEAU. Day spent in cleaning up & resting. Weather fine & sunny. Open air concert by Batt Party.	C.O.
	8th		Tents & bivouacs struck – camp moved to field near RIDGE WOOD.	C.O.
	9th		Day spent in cleaning up & reorganising. Weather wet & stormy. Company organisation carried on during the morning. C.O.'s Inspection in afternoon. Enemy aircraft very active, bombing raids being carried out in the neighbourhood of HALLE BAST. Open air concert by Batt Concert Party & Boxing Competition were held in the evening.	C.O.
IMPERIAL TRENCH	10th		Battalion relieved 11th Queens R.W.S. Regt & the 20th Durham Light Infantry in Support. D Coys moved to DE ZON CAMP.	C.O. I 34.d.85.90
"	11th		Weather unsettled. Battalion remained in support & supplied carrying parties to the 237th Field Coy R.E. Enemy aircraft active, & artillery very active during the night.	C.O.
	12th		Weather continued showery. Morning parties were again supplied. Working parties sent to front line to assist in consolidating trench.	C.O.

Army Form C. 2118.

WAR DIARY
or
INTELLIGENCE SUMMARY   Sheet III

(Erase heading not required.)

Instructions regarding War Diaries and Intelligence Summaries are contained in F. S. Regs., Part II. and the Staff Manual respectively. Title Pages will be prepared in manuscript.

Place	Date	Hour	Summary of Events and Information	Remarks and references to Appendices
IMPERFECT TRENCH	1917 August 13th		Enemy aircraft active throughout the day. Work on front line trench was carried on by working parties at night. Enemy artillery very active during the night, a large number of gas shells being used.	I 36a. 85.9.D
	14th		Battalion was relieved during the afternoon by the 17th Sherwood Foresters, 117th S Bde. Returning to Rest Camp at RIDGE WOOD. Relief complete at 7 p.m.	
RIDGE WOOD	15th		Day spent in cleaning up + resting. At 5.30 p.m. Battalion proceeded by motor lorries from DE ZON CAMP to "G" Camp Battalion at FLETRE. Details marched from HALLE BAST to FLETRE.	
FLETRE	16th		Day spent in reorganising + equipping. Enemy aircraft carried out bombing raid in neighbourhood, bombs being dropped near Officers lines.	
"	17th		Camp was struck + tents erected under cover of hedgerows to prevent observation by enemy aircraft. Battalion inspected by Divisional Commander. After inspection Battalion proceeded on Route March.	
	18th		Battalion inspected by G.O.C. 2nd Army. Remainder of day was spent in recreation.	

WAR DIARY or INTELLIGENCE SUMMARY

Army Form C. 2118.

Sheet IV

Place	Date	Hour	Summary of Events and Information	Remarks and references to Appendices
FLETRE	1917 August 19th		Battalion Church Parade on Batln. Parade Ground. Baths at LA BESACE FARM (X.9a.2.7) were allotted to the Battalion. The undermentioned N.C.O's & men were congratulated by the Commanding Officer on being awarded the MILITARY MEDAL for gallantry & devotion to duty at KLEIN ZILLEBEKE on the 5th August 1917. 1461 Sgt H HARRISON 21149 Pte A.C.J LORD 4784 Cpl G.H.J SPRING 60209 " A GOODLAKE 4659 Pte T LOVELL	CR
	20th		Battalion training. The following work being carried out:- Physical Training under C.S.M. CHEETHAM. Lewis Gun Instruction. Bayonet Fighting. Weather bright & sunny.	CR
	21st		Platoon & Company training during the morning. Specialist training was also carried out & a lecture was given to all officers by Major H.A. ROBINSON, D.S.O. Battalion Route March in afternoon, distance about 6 miles	CR
	22nd		Bath'n in mass for Physical Training under C.S.M CHEETHAM. Coys carried out Bayonet Fighting & the usual Specialist classes were held. The afternoon was spent in cleaning up equipment &c. From 9 – 10.30 pm Coys carried out a short route march.	CR

WAR DIARY or INTELLIGENCE SUMMARY

Army Form C. 2118.

Sheet V

Instructions regarding War Diaries and Intelligence Summaries are contained in F. S. Regs., Part II. and the Staff Manual respectively. Title Pages will be prepared in manuscript.

(Erase heading not required.)

Place	Date	Hour	Summary of Events and Information	Remarks and references to Appendices
FLETRE	1917 August 23rd		Usual training carried out during the morning. Battalion Route March at 2 p.m. Distance about 6 miles.	
"	24th		Usual morning training. Battalion inspected by Commanding Officer, followed by Route March.	
"	25th		Battalion proceeded by march route to TATINGHEM area, halting for the night 25/26th in billets at STAPLE (V.5.c). Distance about 9 miles, time of arrival at STAPLE at 1 p.m.	V.5.c
STAPLE	26th		Battalion left STAPLE at 7.30 a.m. & continued march to TATINGHEM, arriving at billets about 1 p.m. Remainder of day spent in resting.	
"	27th		Weather very wet. Specialist training carried out in billets.	
"	28th		Weather continued wet. Company & Specialist training in billets lectures by Company Commanders.	
"	29th		Battalion on Training Ground. Platoon & Company training being carried out, new attack formation receiving special attention.	

WAR DIARY
or
INTELLIGENCE SUMMARY

Army Form C. 2118.

Sheet VI

Place	Date	Hour	Summary of Events and Information	Remarks and references to Appendices
FATINGHEM Area	August 1917 (30th)		Battalion in Training Ground, usual training being carried out. Lectures were given to Officers + N.C.Os.	C.D.W
	31st		Inspection of 124th Infantry Brigade by the Field Marshal, Commanding-in-Chief. After Inspection the Brigade marched past the Field Marshal, Commanding Chief expressed his entire satisfaction with the smart & soldierly appearance of all ranks, their steadiness on parade and their handling of arms.	C.D.W

CASUALTIES
during action of
31/7/17 - 7/8/17

	Officers	O Ranks
KILLED	2	41
DIED of WOUNDS	1	6
WOUNDED	4	84
MISSING		3
TOTAL	7	134

CASUALTIES
from 8th - 31/8/17

	Officers	O Ranks
KILLED		1
DIED of WOUNDS		
WOUNDED		2
MISSING		
TOTAL		3

STRENGTH during AUGUST

	OFF	OR
MAXIMUM	42	944
MINIMUM	32	840
PRESENT	42	904

C.D.W
2nd Lieut Acting Adjt
for OC Co. Commanding
2/5th Royal Sussex

WAR DIARY *or* **INTELLIGENCE SUMMARY**
(Erase heading not required.)

Army Form C. 2118.

41 Div. SHEET 1 Vol 17

32nd (S) Bn The Royal Fusiliers

Place	Date	Hour	Summary of Events and Information	Remarks and references to Appendices
TATINGHEM	1917 Sept 1st		Battalion in Training. "A" Range at Q.14.d allotted to the Battalion, & the following practices were carried out:— 1. Application (5-rds) 200 yards 2. Rapid (15 rds - 1 m magazine) 200 yards 3. Snap Shooting (5 rds) 300 yards 4. Application (5 rds) 400 yards During the evening the Regtl Band gave a performance in the Gardens at ST OMER.	Sheet 27A S.E. X.10.9.1
	2nd		Battalion behind in Field at X.20.b.3.9. The Divisional Commander travelled ribbons to the following recipients, for gallantry & devotion to duty:— Lt Col W. C. CLARK D.S.O. Capt H. F. WOOD M.C. Bar to M. MEDAL 22333 Pte CASS J 22699 Cpl BARTLETT E L MILITARY MEDAL 22531 Sgt MURCHIE F. G. 38179 L/Cpl BOVINGTON G. 47874 " GRAZIER J. H. 10195 " GRAVES N. 21144 Pte LORD A. J. C. 60204 " GOODLAKE A 38502 " PERKINS W H 9853 " WALKER H	
	3rd		Company & Platoon Training was carried out. Baths were allotted to the Battalion during the morning.	
	4th		The usual Platoon & Company Training was carried out in the morning. A Scheme of Demonstration was received from the G.O.C. Training & completing all units which took part in the parade for the demonstrations in behalf of the 31st Div on the splendid way in which everything was carried out. The Commander in Chief expressed himself as very pleased with all he saw.	

WAR DIARY
or
INTELLIGENCE SUMMARY

Army Form C. 2118.

SHEET II

(Erase heading not required.)

Place	Date	Hour	Summary of Events and Information	Remarks and references to Appendices
TATINGHEM Area	1917 September 5th		Company & Battalion Training on Training Ground. Lewis gun & Scouts practice & specialist training were also carried out. Battalion Sports Meeting was held during the afternoon on Field at X.26.B.O. followed by a concert by the Battalion Party	X.14.9.1. 209
"	6th		Battalion Training under Major H.A. ROBINSON, DSO, MC, for attack against two objectives. Troops in front taking & consolidating the 1st Objective, 2 supporting troops, leap frogging & taking & consolidating the 2nd Objective.	209
"	7th		The Brigade Scheme of Attack was carried out on the Training Ground by the Battalion	209
"	8th		Battalion practised Brigade attack with other Units of the Brigade on the Training Area.	"
"	9th		Battalion attended Brigade Church Parade on Field at X.9 central. After Church Parade the Battalion marched to Field at X.2c.35.45. where the Commanding Officer distributed the knights for the Sports Meeting. Draft of 118 other ranks arrived from 39th & 50th Base Depot	209
"	10th		Practice Attack carried out in conjunction with the other units of the 124th & 122nd Brigades. A counter attack scheme with shelter enemy was arranged. Brigade Forward Command Post, Advanced Dump & R.O.P. were also established. During the afternoon officers visited model of country opposite new Divl Front. W.O & Sergts attended Lecture in R.F.C. Hall LONGUENESSE.	169

Army Form C. 2118.

WAR DIARY
or
INTELLIGENCE SUMMARY
(Erase heading not required.)

SHEET III

Instructions regarding War Diaries and Intelligence Summaries are contained in F. S. Regs., Part II. and the Staff Manual respectively. Title Pages will be prepared in manuscript.

Place	Date	Hour	Summary of Events and Information	Remarks and references to Appendices
TATINGHEM	1917 Septbr 11th		Usual Platoon & Company Training. A New Demonstration of Platoon was given by Divisional Gas Officers. 7 Officers reconnoitred new sector of the line to be taken Over by the Battalion.	X.12.9.1
"	12th		Practice Attack was repeated under same arrangements as for the 10th. Party of 6 Officers reconnoitred new sector of the line. During the afternoon the Second Army Rifle grenade practice ground was allotted to the Battalion.	A.91
"	13th		Companies carried out arms, feet & boot inspections. Rest of the day was spent in voting & recreation.	A.91
"	14th		Battalion commenced to march to the forward area. Route for the day being LONGUENESSE - ARQUES - LE NIEPPE - LES TROIS ROIS - O.26.b - ZUYTPEENE (0.7.a). Distance about 12½ miles. The night 14/15th was spent in billets in the ZUYTPEENE area.	O.7.a. A.91
ZUYTPEENE	15th		March to the forward area continued via BAVIN CHOVE - OXELAERE - O.12 to S.4 - P.7.a.4.9. STEENVOORDE - EECKE - Q.28.59. - THIEUSHOUK (Distance about 13½ miles) Battalion arrived at billets at 4 pm. & the night was spent in THIEUSHOUK district.	W.6.a.5.9 Sheet 27m A.91
THIEUSHOUK	16th		Battalion continued its march to the forward area, halting for the night at MURRUMBIDGEE CAMP, LA CLYTTE. The route for the day being Q.300 - R.25.b. - R.19.d. - BERTHEN - R.16.c - WESTOUTRE - CANADA CORNER - LA CLYTTE. The weather remained bright & clear throughout the march. Draft of 37 O.R. arrived from 39th Staff Base District	N.7.a.6.3 Sheet 28 Sw.
LA CLYTTE				

WAR DIARY or **INTELLIGENCE SUMMARY**

Army Form C. 2118.

Sheet IV

(Erase heading not required.)

Place	Date	Hour	Summary of Events and Information	Remarks and references to Appendices
RIDGE WOOD	1917 September 17th		Battalion moved to RIDGE WOOD by route march, arriving in camp at 11 pm.	N.5a.7.8. Sheet 28 NW
	18th		Concentration of the Brigade was resumed on the night 18th/19th. Battalion moved to the area of CANADA STREET TUNNELS. I Staff marched to CARNARVON CAMP. Battalion Bombing Party gave a performance prior to the Battalion moving to the forward area. Weather clear & bright.	NW
CANADA STREET TUNNELS				
	19th		Battalion remained in position throughout the day. During the night the Battalion moved up to its assembly position for the attack on TOWER HAMLETS	do
	20th		Report on attack attached.	NW
	21st		Day spent in consolidating objectives gained. Enemy artillery very active. Weather fine & bright	NW
	22nd		Battalion holding the line. Consolidation of objectives continued. Enemy artillery & aircraft very active. During the night 22/23rd Battalion was relieved in the line & took over the night at RIDGE WOOD.	NW
RIDGE WOOD	23rd		Day spent in resting & cleaning up. Battalion marched to OUDERDOM & entrained at 5.30 pm for CASTRE. On arrival at CASTRE Battalion marched to LA BREARDE, arriving in billets at 1am. 2nd Lieut R.W. HAMMOND given temp. command of 26th Pm R.F. in vice….	V.5c Sheet 27a NW
CASTRE AREA				

WAR DIARY or INTELLIGENCE SUMMARY

SHEET V

Army Form C. 2118.

Place	Date	Hour	Summary of Events and Information	Remarks and references to Appendices
LA BREARDE	1917 Sept 24th		Day spent in resting & cleaning up.	V 5c. Sheet 27a
"	25th		Congratulatory message received from Divisional Commander, on the way in which the attack on the 20th September 1917 was made, & the determined way in which many strong positions & difficult points were dealt with. The following message was also received from Field Marshal Viscount French "My warmest congratulations & best wishes to all my old comrades". Company organisation & Specialist training was carried out. Baths were allotted to the Battalion	V 5c
"	26th		Weather continued bright & clear. Company & specialist training & reorganisation were continued	"
"	27th		The G.O.C. 124th Brigade inspected the recent drafts. Battalion Transport proceeded by march route to the GHYVELDE area, halting for the night at WORMHOUDT	
"	28th		Weather clear & bright. 41st Division transferred from Second to Fourth Armies. Battalion moved to GHYVELDE by bus, arriving in camp at 6 noon. Remainder of day spent in resting. Enemy aircraft very active at night, bombs being dropped in the vicinity of the camp	

Army Form C. 2118.

WAR DIARY
or
INTELLIGENCE SUMMARY

SHEET VI

(Erase heading not required.)

Instructions regarding War Diaries and Intelligence Summaries are contained in F.S. Regs., Part II. and the Staff Manual respectively. Title Pages will be prepared in manuscript.

Place	Date	Hour	Summary of Events and Information	Remarks and references to Appendices
GHYVELDE	1917 September 29th		Inspection by Divisional Commander. Company & Specialist Training. Bathing in the sea during the afternoon. Enemy aircraft active at night.	D.21.C.80.90 SHEET 19 A.M.
	30th		Battalion Church Parade on Parade Ground. Remainder of day spent in rest & recreation. Enemy aircraft active at night.	

CASUALTIES during action of 19 - 22/9/1917

	Officers	Other Ranks
KILLED		35
DIED of WOUNDS		5
WOUNDED	10	224
MISSING	4	29
TOTAL	14	293

✱ 3 since died of wounds, 1 killed

STRENGTH during SEPTEMBER

	Off.	O.R.
MAXIMUM	41	954
MINIMUM	25	666
PRESENT	25	666

R E P O R T

on

OPERATIONS, 20th to 23rd September, 1917.

32nd (S) Bn The ROYAL FUSILIERS.

1. CONCENTRATION.
The Battalion marched from TATINGHEM (St OMER area) to MURRUMBIDGEE CAMP, LA CLYTTE, in three consecutive days.
17th. Moved to RIDGE WOOD.
Night 18th/19th moved to MOUNT SORREL area, digging in about 500 yards W. of CANADA STREET TUNNELS (Bde Hdqrs) - Battalion Hdqrs in TUNNELS.

At dusk on 18th evening enemy put creeping barrage, mostly 4.2 and 5.9 H.E., across the area, causing 20 casualties, including the Battn Signalling Officer (Wounded).

2. ASSEMBLY.
Night 19th/20th Battalion moved into Assembly Position in file along CLEMSONS LANE to SHREWSBURY FOREST, its front resting on the road running North from just West of LOWER STAR POST, its right being immediately behind LOWER STAR POST and its left on the road 250 yards North of that point. Assembly completed 1 hour before Zero, with two casualties.

3. DISPOSITION.
In support on the Right of the Brigade Sector, 50 yds in rear of the 10th "Queens" (the attacking Battalion of the Right Sector) whose waves were closed up so as to occupy 75 yds depth from front to rear of the Battalion.
The 17th K.R.R.C., 39th Division, on the right, the 26th Royal Fusiliers, supporting the 21st K.R.R.C, on the left.
Battalion disposed as follows:-
"A" Coy (right) and "B" Coy (left) in front line with "D" Coy (right) and "C" Coy (left) in support.
All Coys, with 2 platoons in front wave and 1 platoon on 2nd wave, each wave being a line of sections in file.
The whole Battalion closed up to a depth of 75 yards.

4. THE ADVANCE.
At Zero hour, 5.40 am, (Summer time), the Battalion advanced in close formation immediately behind the 10th "Queens", thus escaping the enemy barrage which dropped a few minutes later well behind the Battalion - the assembly having been carried out without being observed by the enemy's forward posts.
There was no obstacle to the advance in the first 200 yards, but at about that point very heavy machine gun fire was opened from JAVA DRIVE on the left front from shell holes and from the trench opposite the centre, causing very heavy casualties amongst the 10th "Queens" and also amongst the Battalion.

(1)

4. The Advance (Contd)

The attack was definitely held up in the centre and the majority of the officers of the Battalion became casualties, including the Acting Adjutant and two of the Company Commanders, a third being hit but remaining at duty.

The 10th "Queens" Ceased to be a fighting unit but "A" Company, under 2nd Lt. CHRISTIE, pushed on on the right, and "B" Company, under the C.S.M., got forward on the left, moving out of the Battalion Sector.

This relieved the pressure on the centre and the whole line was enabled to progress, though the check had lost the Brigade the benefit of the barrage.

In spite of this there was no serious opposition encountered between the RED and the BLUE LINES, though the enemy Machine Gun fire and sniping from the opposing ridge was heavy and accurate.

By 9 am the BLUE LINE was captured but the units were extremely disorganised, and owing to the heavy casualties, which amounted to about 50% of the Battalion, it was found impossible, in face of the M.G. fire to organise a further advance.

The Battalion had captured the first two Objectives (which had been assigned to the attacking Battalion in front of it) and was unfitted for any further effort beyond holding the ground gained.

At about this period the 17th K.R.R.C. on the right were re-inforced by a battalion of the Cheshire Regt. and a portion of the latter, seeing how thin our line was, took up their position on the left of our right party.

A portion of the Left Company of the Battalion had moved so far across to that flank that they finally dug themselves in on the opposing slope, about 200 yards beyond the BASSEVILLE BEEK, on the extreme left of the Bde Sector, together with a party of the 26th Royal Fusiliers, while parties of the 21st K.R.R.C. and 18th K.R.R.C. were behind them West of the BASSEVILLE BEEK.

Thereafter the Machine Gun fire of the enemy, partly from the opposing slope and especially from the rather low ground opposite the Division on the right, became, and remained, very serious, making movement even by indivuals very hazardous, and effectually preventing any movement by bodies of men.

The sniping too was very accurate.

At about 4 pm and 6 pm the enemy were reported to be massing opposite our front for a counter-attack, but our S.O.S. Barrage was prompt and prevented any developments.

The Brigade was re-inforced by the 123rd Brigade and orders were given for the 23rd Middlesex to assemble on the left of the BLUE LINE and attacked the GREEN LINE at 9.30 am on the 21st in a S.S.E. direction.

Great difficulty was experienced in assembling on the somewhat vague line then being held in the face of continual Machine Gun fire and increased shell fire. The advance was begun, several dugouts were captured and cleared, but after about 300 yards the advance was definitely held up by Machine Gun fire from undamaged concrete dugouts and from trenches.

4. The Advance (Contd)

During the morning very effective Machine Gun fire was brought to bear on the opposing ridge from 8 Machine Guns posted just behind our RED LINE and also from rifles in the BLUE LINE, but by noon the attempt was abandoned and the BLUE LINE became again the ultimate line of the ground captured in these operations, and was held by mixed elements of the two Brigades.

The Battalion was relieved on the nights 22nd/23rd and 23rd/24th.

5. ARTILLERY

(a) OUR BARRAGE.

At Zero hour the barrage gave the impression of being some 350 yards away instead of 150 yards, and in fact the attacking troops being held up near the start, never got really under it. The distance of the smoke and dust-cloud was undoubtedly due in part to the fact that no H.E. was observable in the "A" Barrage, and this employment of a shrapnel "A" barrage appeared to be ineffectual in keeping down the fire of the forward enemy Machine Guns.

(b) S.O.S. BARRAGE.

This was exceedingly prompt and effectual.

(c) ENEMY BARRAGE.

Started well behind our assembled troops and was only spasmodic during the whole of the 20th.

On the 20th night and during the whole of the following two days and nights it was very heavy on the area from the original Front Line back to the 18 pounder line, with occasional heavy bursts on the forward area.

6. TRENCH MORTAR BATTERY.

Did not come into action. They might be very useful if brought up well after the advance when there would be a better chance of the teams, with their ammunition, arriving more or less in-tact. They could then be most usefully employed in barraging Strong Points against which it would be impossible to employ a fresh artillery barrage without a good many hours delay.

7. MACHINE GUNS.

(a) OURS. The Machine Gun Barrage fire was, of course, unobservable during the advance, but during the consolidation of the BLUE LINE it appears to have been a valuable addition to the Artillery Protective Barrage.

The Machine Guns allotted to the Battalions reached a splendid position immediately behind the RED LINE and were extremely useful in harrassing the enemy on the opposing ridge, at a range of 950 yards.- During the 21st they found many targets on that ridge and were of great assistance.

(b) ENEMY. His Machine Guns in the forward line, both in dugouts and in trenches, were unaffected by the shrapnel/barrage and the morale of the teams

7. MACHINE GUNS (Contd)

was up to a high standard - they fought their guns until flanking parties had got well round their positions.

During the whole action enemy Machine Guns were very active from the opposing slope, and one gun firing from opposite the next sector on the right was able to sweep the whole of the Battalion position, including the low ground around the BASSEVILLE BEEK and the high ground about the RED LINE and behind. This gun was never put out of action.

8. SNIPING AND RIFLE FIRE.

(a) OURS. Sniping poor, great lack of individual effort. Rifle fire was used by groups very largely, particularly after reaching the BLUE LINE. So much so that, while waiting for further supplies of S.A.A., the main party on the right was using enemy rifles and ammunition of which they had captured large quantities, and fired some thousands of rounds in assisting to cover the advance of the 123rd Brigade.

There was abundant evidence that whenever the enemy became exposed to rifle fire his resistance ceased at once.

(b) ENEMY. Sniping good, continuous and very harassing. The individual courage and determination of the enemy when in a fairly good protected position, was very well exemplified by this.

Rifle fire of other description apparently nil.

9. COMMUNICATIONS.

(a) TELEPHONIC: The Brigade Forward Station at R.P.1 was never out of touch with the Bde Hdqrs for more than a few minutes. The wires were cut by shell-fire a good many times, but the work done by the linesmen was prompt and courageous and deserves special mention.

(b) A POWER BUZZER was in action soon after the post was established and was a valuable auxiliary.

(c) VISUAL was used only on the extreme left of the Brigade Sector, where one of the main parties of the Battalion was. No signallers reached the right of the BLUE LINE.

(d) RUNNERS. Most valuable and efficient. Continuous communication was maintained with all parties after the attainment of the 2nd Objective, and the work done by this branch of the Battalion was of outstanding merit.

(e) WIRELESS was not used.

10. **SUPPLIES.**
S.A.A., rations and water were sent up by the Brigade, and most of them reached Battn Hdqrs and were distributed to parties in front. But the shelling of back areas was particularly heavy on the 21st and 22nd and the conducting of carrying parties presented very great difficulties.

The forward Battalion dumps were not used, partly owing to the shortage of men available for sending back, and partly because as this Battalion had not been in the line before the 20th there were none who could be depended on to guide a party to the right spot. Shortage of men was a hampering factor on every occasion of any sory throughout the operations.

11. **MEDICAL.**
The work of the R.A.M.C. bearers appeared to be very good in spite of the large number of cases to be dealt with. The evacuation of the wounded was made comparatively easy by the fact that about 70 per cent of the casualties must have occurred before reaching the RED LINE.

In the forward area great use was made of enemy prisoners as bearers, who, generally speaking, behaved very well in this respect.

I would suggest, however, that a practice be made both by Battalions and the R.A.M.C. of carrying and erecting a number of small sign-posts to indicate the direction to and position of R.A.Ps and Bearer Relay Posts.

12. **CASUALTIES.**

		Officers	O.Ranks
(a)	KILLED	-	35
	DIED OF WOUNDS	-	5
	WOUNDED	10	224
	MISSING	4	29 x
		14	293

Of the total sent up 77% officers became casualties and 60% other ranks.

x   Of the 4 Officers "Missing" 1 was subsequently Killed and the other 3 Died of Wounds.

Of the 29 Other Ranks "Missing", 6 have since been reported Killed in Action, and 1 Wounded. 2 of the Wounded have died.

(b) At least 70% of the total casualties occurred in the attack on the RED LINE and were caused by bullet wounds.

13. POINTS suggested by the OPERATIONS.

(a) BARRAGE. 18 Pounder Shrapnel is ineffectual in dealing with M.G. Emplacements and has little moral effect.

It also produces very little "line" for the leading waves to follow. The impression produced on me personally at Zero hour was that, although I was ahead of my Battalion and within 70 yards of the leading wave of the front Battalion, the barrage was over 300 yards in front of me.

Suggested that "A" Barrage be entirely H.E., and good deal of shrapnel being used in "B" Barrage to catch enemy retiring from forward posts across the open.

(b) RIFLE FIRE. Was good when carried out by parties under an officer or senior N.C.O., but individual effort is lacking, men being too apt to lie in shell holes with their heads well down, not realizing that every British sniper will assist in Neutralizing enemy sniping.

(c) GRENADES. Men have not learnt the value of this weapon against M.G. Emplacements and Strong Points; the want of realism in training is partly responsible.

(d) LEADERSHIP AND INITIATIVE. This is the pivot of the whole question of success in such operations. The importance of it has not been overlooked in training but it is clear that too much attention cannot be paid to it. The difficulty of the advance was enhanced enormously from the time when 14 out of 18 officers became casualties by the want of confidence of the N.C.Os in themselves and of the men in their N.C.Os.

(e) MINOR TACTICS. A great deal of training has been devoted to the principle of flank attacks on emplacements and strong points, and this was carried out in practice on several occasions with complete and immediate success; but time and lives are still lost through it not being universally applied.

(f) The formation was too dense. It would appear impracticable to attempt, once the advance has begun and if any opposition is encountered, to open out two Battalions from a total depth of 150 yards or so to their proper depth and at the same time retain efficient organization and control.

Lt. Col. Comdg
32nd (S) Bn The Royal Fusiliers.

Army Form C. 2118.

WAR DIARY
or
INTELLIGENCE SUMMARY

(Erase heading not required.)

Sheet I Vol 18

32nd (S) Bn Royal Fusiliers

Place	Date	Hour	Summary of Events and Information	Remarks and references to Appendices
GHYVELDE "B" Camp	1917 Oct 1st		During the morning Battalion carried out Platoon & Company Drill Musketry. Fire control in afternoon. Training carried out during afternoon. Weather bright & clear. Enemy aircraft active, a further 3 bombs being dropped in the neighbourhood. Draft of 283 O.R. arrived from 39th Inf Base Depot.	D 21C. 80.90 SHEET 19
"	2nd		Weather bright & clear. Organisation of new drafts. Battn on Northern Training Area (West). Platoon & Coy Drill & Specialist training being carried out. Enemy aircraft active at night.	"
"	3rd		Manual Training on Southern Training Area (West). Weather continues fine.	"
"	4th		Rifle Range allotted to the Battalion, the following practices being carried out. 1st SC 5 rounds Application at 200 yards. 2nd SC 10 rounds Rapid at 200 yards.	"
"	5th		Usual Company & Specialist Training carried out on Southern Training Area (East). 1 Officer joined from Base.	"
"	6th		Battalion warned from GHYVELDE to COXYDE BAINS (WILTSHIRE CAMP) to relieve the 11th East Lancs Regt in the Reserve Battalion sector of the coast defence. Relief complete at 7 p.m.	X 16 central SHEET 11.
COXYDE BAINS	7th		Battalion Church Parade. Afternoon spent in rest & recreation. Weather clear & bright. 6 Officers joined from Base	"

18.

WAR DIARY or INTELLIGENCE SUMMARY

32nd (?) Bn Royal Fusiliers Sheet II

Army Form C. 2118.

Place	Date	Hour	Summary of Events and Information	Remarks and references to Appendices
COXYDE BAINS	1917 Oct 8th		Physical Training & Bayonet Fighting. Platoon Drill & Specialist Training was carried out. The Commanding Officer & 2 Officers from Army reconnoitered the O.D.B. defence sector.	X 1 to centre
"		9	Usual Training. The C.O. lectured to all new Officers. Sandbagging of huts carried out.	"
"		10	Lecture to all ranks on Outposts. Outpost drill in putting out a small outpost line. Sandbagging of huts continued.	"
"		11	Baths at ST IDESBALDE allotted to Battalion. Specialist & Company Training continued.	"
"		12	Practical Outpost Work & Lectures. Lewis Gun Teams carried out firing practice. Specialist Training in their new arms.	"
"		13	Lectures by Company Commanders on Trench Routine & Gas. Physical Training, Musketry, Lewis Gun & Rifle Grenade instruction carried out. MILITARY MEDALS awarded by the X.h Corps Commander to the undermentioned for devotion to duty during the attack on the 20th Sept 1917. 63178 Pte C.A. MUCHMORE. 60190 7/6 E ROBINSON	"

WAR DIARY or INTELLIGENCE SUMMARY

Army Form C. 2118.

Sheet III 32nd (S) Bn Royal Fusiliers

(Erase heading not required.)

Place	Date	Hour	Summary of Events and Information	Remarks and references to Appendices
COXYDE BAINS	1917 Oct. 14th		Battalion Church Parade in Convent Hall, WILTSHIRE CAMP. Remainder of day spent in resting	X.1.b central
In the Line	15		Battalion relieved the 11th Bn "Queens" R.W.S. Regt in the Right Bn Sector of the Front line. Tommy artillery active during relief. Details proceeded to CORNWALL CAMP. OOST DUNKERKE. Weather clear & bright. The undermentioned were awarded honours by the XVth Corps Commander for gallantry & devotion to duty during the attack on 20.9.17. MILITARY MEDALS 8940 A/CSM T DAVIES 22195 Sgt J H ROBBINS 16783 Pte J CRAMB 9613 Sgt C H HISCOKE 49646 Pte W HORNE 9643 L/Cpl W A OXENHAM 49617 Pte A G CRAMB 22191 L/Cpl E PEGGS 60224 Pte F G CLARKE 49616 Pte R J COLE 8962 2/Sgt J KELLY BAR TO MILITARY MEDALS 38179 T/Sgt C.G.H. BOVINGTON 54945 Pte C BAYLEY	B.H.Q M 20.B.84
	16th		Weather bright & clear. Our aircraft very active. Enemy artillery active especially on back areas. D.C.M awarded by the Field Marshall Commanding-in-Chief to 52677 A/CSM C GORMAN for remarkable bravery & coolness during attack on 20.9.17.	

WAR DIARY
or
INTELLIGENCE SUMMARY

(Erase heading not required.)

Army Form C. 2118.

32nd (1) Bn Royal Fusiliers   Sheet IV

Place	Date	Hour	Summary of Events and Information	Remarks and references to Appendices
In the Line	1917 Oct 17th		Enemy Trench Mortars active on CLOSE SUPPORT. Our aircraft very active, especially with Machine Guns against enemy lines. Enemy artillery very active, the troops near BHQ receiving special attention.	M 20 L 8 4 AA
"	18th		Enemy Trench Mortars active, causing casualties 1 O.R. Killed & 2 O.R. Wounded. Enemy artillery continued active - our artillery carried out retaliation shoots. Our aircraft very active over enemy lines.	AA
"	19th		Our aircraft active dropping bombs on enemy defence north OOST-DUNKERKE ROAD was very heavily shelled by enemy. Enemy T.M. active, shelling 2 O.R. Wire defences strengthened on both flanks.	AA "
"	20th		Artillery on both sides very active. Wiring parties sent out. The Field Marshal Commanding in Chief awarded the following honours to the undermentioned officers. BAR TO D.S.O. Lt Col W.C. CLARK, D.S.O. D.S.O. 2nd Lt M.I. CHRISTIE BAR TO M.C. 2nd Lt W.P. TROTTER M.C. MILITARY CROSS Capt R.W. HAMMOND " H. DIPPIE 2nd Lt A.C. DAVY " M.C.B. TODD	"

WAR DIARY or INTELLIGENCE SUMMARY

32nd (1) Bn Royal Fusiliers Sheet V

(Erase heading not required.)

Place	Date	Hour	Summary of Events and Information	Remarks and references to Appendices
In the line	1917 Oct 21		Artillery duel continued. Enemy shelled the vicinity of OOST DUNKERKE. Shells falling around Details Camp & HQ. Wiring carried on.	M.20.b. 84
"	Oct 22		Artillery below the usual activity on both sides. Improvement of trenches on carried out. Wire defences again strengthened.	"
"	23		Enemy artillery fairly quiet. The Battalion was relieved by the 10th Bn Queens R.W.S. Regt on night 23/24th commencing at 12.30 a.m. On relief the Battn marched to OOST-DUNKERKE (X.3.a.9.1.) & took new YORKSHIRE CAMP (X.3.a.9.1.)	"
YORKSHIRE CAMP	24		Day spent in cleaning up & resting.	X.3.a.9.1.
"	25		Bath at YORKSHIRE CAMP allotted to the Battn. Major H.A. ROBINSON, D.S.O. awarded the Bar to his D.S.O.	"
"	26		Company & Specialist Training carried out. YORKSHIRE CAMP shelled with H.V. shells. 2 O.R. being wounded	"
"	27		Usual training carried out.	"

Army Form C. 2118.

WAR DIARY
or
INTELLIGENCE SUMMARY

Sheet VI

(Erase heading not required.)

32nd (J) Bn Royal Fusiliers

Place	Date	Hour	Summary of Events and Information	Remarks and references to Appendices
TETEGHEM	1917 Octr 28th		Battalion relieved by 7th Bn Seaforth Highlanders (9th Division) & conveyed from COXYDE to TETEGHEM Area by lorries.	T.15.b 2.3 SHEET 19
"	29		Company organisation & training carried out	"
"	30		Usual training	"
"	31st		"	"
			Casualties during the month	
			KILLED 3 O.R.	
			WOUNDED 6 O.R.	
			Strength during October	

	Officers	O.R.
MAXIMUM	41	1004
MINIMUM	27	983
PRESENT	41	1004

R. C. J. Edge
Capt & Adjt
for Lt Col comdg
32nd (J) Bn The Royal Fusiliers

www.ingramcontent.com/pod-product-compliance
Lightning Source LLC
Chambersburg PA
CBHW081542160426
43191CB00011B/1816